10-6.08

Rev. Ann Breswell

THROUGH
THE FIRE – GOD

Pat K. Braswell

ACKNOWLEDGEMENT

For the Author of my life that has given me the mind and strength to write this book. Who gave me the courage to face difficult times of the past and write with joy to have seen where He brought me from.

I have never written a book before but I know that God has given to me. Many people have gone through similar situations, and will identify with me that He is more than able to keep you in the fires.

Romans 3:20 declares, *"Now unto him that is able to do exceeding abundantly above all that we ask or think, according to the power that worketh in us."*

May you be strengthened, receive new hope and reach your destiny in God as you read this book, "Through The Fires - God."

DEDICATION

To my Heavenly Father who has brought me "through all the fires" and made me strong in my faith. He showed me that "His grace and strength" is sufficient for every need and He is really all I need.

To my mom and dad who are rejoicing in Heaven and waiting on the rest of us to come home.

To my husband, my true love of forty years, my "chocolate drops." (Most beautiful eyes).

To my first child which I will meet in Heaven and that caused me to understand very early in life that God has a perfect plan.

To my two sons, Ken and Jeff and beautiful daughter, Gina.

Last, but certainly not least, my eight grandchildren (sunshines). Lauren, Shelby, Corey, Chandler, Sydney, Sophie, Ashton, and Ethan. They make my life full to overflowing…..

CONTENTS

INTRODUCTION

I was born in Statesboro, Georgia, on September 29, 1948, in the Bulloch County Hospital. I was the first of five children my Mom and Dad would have. My life has been a continual through-the-fire experience that would prepare me for the call I would later receive as a Minister of the Gospel.

To begin as a small country girl and become a daughter of the Most High God still amazes me. His love and care for me at the age of eight and right on through would later prove just how much He cared. No matter where you are today in your walk with God, His grace and love is available.

Isn't it wonderful how God will take someone who is not known or even noticed by people that pass them every day and bring them to the front to meet the challenges of today? It is not unusual for God, you know! From the beginning of time, you will find men and women in His Word who have faced unbelievable odds, endured long painful trials, fires of the breath of the enemy, but God stood them up to tell others that HE IS ABLE.

My prayer is that as you read through the pages of this book, that the Spirit of the Lord will touch you, give a new strength and courage to carry on, even if it seems impossible. You may have already faced some things in your life and wondered, as I did, how did I make it through that?

IT WAS HIM .... He is molding and shaping us into beautiful vessels fit for His greatness. Be prepared to be broken, crushed, and burned in the fires of His furnace if you are going to be effective in your life to touch others. Pure gold shining in the face of the enemy. Praise the Lord for His Greatness..... be uplifted and strengthened as you read the book, Through The Fires – God.

CHAPTER 1:

EARLY DAYS OF MY LIFE

How do I begin? I was born on September 29, 1948 to a family who was very poor. My dad's name was Wesley and my mother's name was Carleen. I have two brothers, Clinton and Glenn, and had two sisters, Shelby and Vickey. My sister Shelby passed on December 24, 1990. I will tell you about her later on in my story. My dad worked on a dairy farm and drove the milk truck back and forth to Savannah to Starland Dairies Company and also worked on the farm, while mom worked along side of my dad.

I remember when mom finally got a job in Statesboro at the Braswell's Food Company to help meet the demands of a growing family. Tired and worn from the hard work, and little pay, but not any real complaint. As I think back to those days I can still smell the aroma of jams, jellies and preserves on her clothes.

They worked hard to provide for us; they would come in from the fields or plant so tired from the day of labor. We did not have the resources and advantages some others were blessed with. Have you often wondered why it seems some people have all the blessings and others seemingly have all the hard breaks in life?

Some people have everything at their disposal, whatever they put their hands to just seems to add to things already that they have. It is not that God is an unjust God, it is just that some things will make you shine brighter for the destiny that is out before you. You will either walk in your destiny like Joseph and rejoice and know that God has everything under control or begin very bitter and resentful.

Trials are not there to hurt us, but to *mold*, *shape* and *define* who we really are. When you look at it in the light of God's Word, then you know *Romans 8:28, "And we know that all things work together for good to those that love God, to them who are the called according to his purpose." God's Word is truth*............... I had learned that in the Scriptures at a very young age. That is why I write to tell you He is the God that brought me through.

There are many things that I did not remember as a child, but I would later come to realize they had been suppressed and would come back to trouble me in my adult life. But, there are good days of memories. I would run down the road and around the old dirt road to my grandmother's where there was a joy. At her home she would make homemade chocolate pudding, (no one could make it like grandmother) and the smell in the air was so rich. She would let me watch her while she made it, and lick the spoon afterward. What a real treat for a small child with a lot of troubling things on her mind. (Some things I would never share until later in my life as a young married woman.)

Grandmother would let me spend the night at her house and, what excitement! She would put us on the floor and bring out the old feather bed and would put layers of blankets on top of us in cold whether and we would snuggle up under those covers. My sisters and I would giggle and tell stories half of the night, fall asleep to wake up the next morning with the smell of bacon cooking, grits, lots of scrambled eggs, and homemade biscuits with the jellies. What a retreat for a small child, with precious memories to carry me through!

I also remember the days when grandpa would have what we called down in the South, "hog killing day." He would get the big old boilers out and light up the fires. You could hear the rumbles and cracking of the fat lighter wood as it would roar.

My grandpa would kill the hogs, make sausage, pork chops, and ribs, then take the hams and shoulders cure them in the old smokehouse. I can still hear the voices of my grandparents and my mother working to finish up the day.

My grandmother would let me spend the night at her house after we had finished the day of working on the farm and as the sun would go down, I would gather up the eggs for her and bring them in.

She would begin to prepare the meal that night which would consist of fresh fried pork chops, rice and tomatoes, and then crisp fried cornbread as we would set the table and fill the quart jars up with ice. My grandparents had a very long table with the long benches fifteen at least would be around that table. We would sit and listen to the adults as they would talk about the things that went on that day and we would pray. My grandpa was not a very outspoken man, but you knew that he loved his wife, family and God.

My grandparents and mom went to Church in Statesboro. My mom would take me along to the Old Institute Street Church of God to experience such great demonstrations of God's glory on their faces. Oh! The joy they had as the saints of God.

My dad came to know the Lord as his personal Savior when a Man of God moved to Statesboro to become the

Pastor of that local church. His name was Reverend Houston Odum. He was a true Man of God that came to our home in the country. We did not have much to eat, just rice and tomatoes, sometimes black-eyed peas and maybe cornbread. The man of God sat down at the table with my family and ate as if we were eating T-Bone steak, baked potatoes and a big green salad, with chocolate delight for dessert.

The love of God oozed out of him in his meek, humble spirit as he shared with my Dad and Mom about the love of God and His desire to save him. We went to Church on the following Sunday and gave his life to the Lord. It was not an easy road, because many trials were yet to come.

Many other memories flood my mind as I write: how my father was such a great landscaper, anything he touched would turn green and he would plant beautiful trees and flowers in the yard. The yards would be the envy of neighbors who could only dream that theirs could be that pretty. The smell of the honeysuckle bushes, the white granddaddy graybeard bush and the red roses. My dad was not only a great landscaper, but God had given him the great ability to build.

He did not have to look at plans or drawings, but with just a thought in his head and he could build it. He and my mom took such great pride in whatever they did and instilled it in us. Their motto was, "what ever you do is worth doing it right."

My earthly father was a good provider and worked hard from daylight to dark, but could not seem to deal with the issues in his own life. They were exposed every time there was something that did not go right. It could have been on the job, on the farm, in the home, or even in the daily drive home.

His anger was an unmanageable generational curse that needed to have been dealt with. He could not express his emotions and say "I love you." He could not fulfill what a small child needs growing up. The father that should have been able to give us security was dealing with his own insecurities and demons. It was at this time my Heavenly Father became the one I would talk with, cry to and know that He was there for me. He loved me unconditionally, with no strings attached.

I remember as if it were yesterday, when I was only eleven years old, dad came home that night angry about something that had not gone right that day. My mom would always receive the blunt end of all of this, and I when I became a little older it was clear to me. My two sisters and I slept in the same bed, and I remember trying to keep them quiet while the anger was raging.

That night as our windows were open to feel the cool air into the bedroom, I looked up into the darkness of the night and saw the stars shining so bright, asking God to change the things that were happening. He calmed my fears, but as a small child, I did not have the understanding of the real enemy we were dealing with.

Those demons would come out during the night and control him to the point where he would become so sick after these things happened, you could hear vomiting and crying. God would send a man to help my father in more ways than one.

Brother Odum was very instrumental in helping my dad to get a job at the new plant that opened in Statesboro. It was called J.P. Stevens Carpet Mill. My dad went from almost nothing to a having a very good salary on his job. Dad was beginning to make more money, so we moved from the country to a little house on Mulberry Street in Statesboro, and God's protecting hands were there.

We were excited about our new little house where we three girls had a room of our own and the boys and mom and dad their own rooms, too. We were in our room getting prepared for bed, turned off the light and in the darkness of night, there was a shadow of a man standing at the window. He walked around the side of house and then came back to the widow where we were. (I do not know what he had planned in his mind for that night,) but God protected us from the plan of the enemy.

HE WILL CARRY US THROUGH THE FIRES TO REACH OUR DESTINY.......... WHATEVER THE ENEMY HAS PLANNED, IT WILL BE CANCELLED IN THE FACE OF GOD.

My first real encounter with God, besides the night I got saved and knew he had His hand on my life, was when I was fourteen. On a Wednesday night prayer meeting at the Church, Sister Odum felt led by the Lord to have every young person come to the front, and hold a lit candle.

She prayed over the youth that God would direct us in our personal relationship with Him, that our families would know Him and that God would bring the right young man or woman into our lives to marry. Even though we were still young, Sister Odum had a spiritual understanding that, with God's help, we needed the right person to spend the rest of our lives with. She came to me and began to pray and there was a prophecy which came forth to me stating God was going to use me to be a light in the darkness.

I can still see the candle I was holding in my hand, still burning while the other's candles went out. (I did not have a clear understanding then that God would later call me to be an Evangelist to reach those that were in that darkness.) My light would shine brightly and God would be with me to stand no matter what came my way. (I did not understand the fullness of all that I would have to go through, tested by many fiery trials.)

It was only a year later I would meet the man of my life. In the Spring of 1964, we were having a gospel sing at the church and the young man that liked me, invited this friend to church with him. When I saw him that night, my breath felt as if had been taken away (I was the ripe old age of fifteen and a half). My prayers and those of Sister Odum were being answered right before my eyes.

My dad was not thrilled like I was about the thought of a young, handsome guy with black hair, dark skin and the most beautiful chocolate drops eyes that you have ever seen, looking or entertaining the thought of dating his daughter. (I called him my "chocolate drops" because they looked like Hershey Kisses.) When I was finally able to go on a date my dad informed to be home by 10:00 and we would not even get out of Church until 9:00 sometime. I was in love and wanted to be with him and tell him my heart.

He came into the Church and into my heart. It is so true "it was love at first sight." Rondy was and is the love of my life and we have just celebrated 40 years of marriage on June 4th, 1967.

Our marriage has not always been a "bed of roses"; many thorns of fiery trials came our way. Married on June 4th, 1967, and had orders for Vietnam on July 13th, 1967. Rondy remained there until the following year.

Here I was, a young bride in love and now without her love. How do you make it through the fiery trial of loneliness, overwhelmed by missing the very thing you had prayer for? For endless days I would wait on the mailman to come with a letter, and there were nights I would cry myself to sleep, feeling the darkness all around me without him. Even in the young days of our married life, I learned the only answer is in Christ. You trust Him completely and know He is a faithful God that did not bring you this far to let you down.

My family and I would be glued to the TV and night after night we would wait to hear the latest concerning the Vietnam war. I constantly prayed protection around him where ever he was and that God would show Himself strong for my beloved. Little do we understand when we are younger the importance of the prayers of the saints of God over our lives. I remember a Man of God preaching a sermon entitled, "Thank God For The Things He Kept Us From."

If Heaven was opened up and we could see the many things the enemy had devised against our lives and loved ones, how God's protecting hand reached down in it all, we would praise Him more than we ever have. The song, "Someone Is Praying For You," would later take on a new meaning as I understood the prayers I had prayed over him.

I will never forget the day when we received word that he was returning home. The plane landed in Savannah, Georgia and I was standing with my mom and dad, my eyes fixed only for the one that I had long to see. I was waiting to feel his embrace and hear the words "I have missed you and love you." God had brought in through the war and safely home to me.

In July 1968, still having several months left before he got out of the Army, we moved to Hephzibah, Georgia. During those last months of 1968, I was expecting our first baby. I was so happy and feeling like everything was going my way, but it was in the ending of my three and half months when I began to hemorrhage uncontrollably and was taken to the hospital where after an hour or a little later I lost our baby. My heart once again faced a new trail in my life, this was only the beginning of many things to come.

I believe only God can fully understand the emptiness a woman feels when life has been conceived, and new life is inside, and the grief one feels when it is taken away unexpectedly. That is when God, "works all things for our good." Joseph said it best in *Genesis 50:20, "But as for you, ye thought evil against me; but God meant it unto good, to bring to pass, as it is this day, to save much people alive." BUT GOD MEANT IT UNTO GOOD, TO BRING TO PASS* .... *An expected end.*

God brought me through that trial, and one year later on September 30, 1969, our first son Kenny was born. He was already showing his independence by being birthed a little over one hour after my birthday. He was my pride and joy, he filled a void in my life that was so real from the loss of the first child. The new life that was inside of me brought on new beginnings and I felt the flutter of his life inside me a few months later while in Church He is talented, gifted to sing and played the piano when he was only three years old. When he became a young man of thirty, God poured over 25 songs into him.

Kenny's life would forever be changed when he turned seven years old, and our lives as parents turned into sorrow when years later we learned he had been molested by someone (not a family member) during a gathering of my family at Christmas. Kenny was left with deep wounds which only God could heal and make whole. He would receive strength and go on, but in his mind a battle was raging that would later get out of control in his teen years and married life.

He fought against a spirit that warred inside of him. In God's presence, he would give it to God and His mind would be at peace. The very thing God delivers you from must be turned away from. All images, people, and distractions must be given to God every day of our lives. That is why it is important that you pray, read the Word of God and know that He is your deliverer.

He met a young Christian woman that experienced what I did, "love at first sight" with him. She would hold onto God knowing that he was the one for her life.

They had two years of engagement, and were to be married on February 26, 1994; this brought relief to me as his mother. I can still see the look in his eyes as they were driving off for their honeymoon; somewhere in the back of my mind and heart I cried.

I knew the enemy was not done yet, and he would try to devour the seed of Kenny's marriage through lies, jeers and mocking. BUT WHO HAS THE LAST WORD, GOD...... IT IS NOT OVER TILL GOD SAYS IT IS OVER!!!!

Out of that marriage came three wonderful gifts from God. My first grandson was named Shelby. My son loved my sister and in honor of her, named his new son Shelby Ryan. Life seemed to be getting better and better for them. God had such awesome things to give them, and destiny was laid out before them, as God does for every one of us. We ultimately choose which way we will go.

The two were such a dynamic team of musicians and would honor God and would lead the congregation into true worship, and God's glory. The devil does not like it when we are released to honor the King. He will try to come steal our songs of victory from us.

Kenny began to entertain the lies of the enemy that he was not and never could be the man of the home, and surely would not be what God wanted. After several years of marriage, our son left his wife and three precious gifts, and ended up in another lifestyle. He has not returned home, and is still a prodigal son, but the Heavenly Father is waiting on him.

My husband and I, are looking forward to the day of his glorious deliverance, peace of mind and restoration of our son. We have the promise of God that he will bring our wayward children home. As a mom who loves her children, I am waiting for the phone call.

Can you imagine the lies of the enemy we as mothers have to face? The accusations Satan is so good at providing? "If you had done this or that; all your training, prayers and fasting are all in vain. How could you birth a child like that?" But he is a liar. In fact, the Bible says in John 8:44, *"Ye are of your father the devil, and the lusts of your father ye will do. He was a murderer from the beginning, and abode not in the truth, because there is no truth in him. When he speaketh a lie, he speaketh of his own: for he is a liar, and the father of it."*

I do not know all the reason for things that come our way in life, but I am sure of one thing, *"The LORD is my rock, and my fortress, and my deliverer; my God, my strength, in whom I will trust; my buckler, and the horn of my salvation, and my high tower."* Psalm 18:2.

Our marriage has endured many trials, from the trauma our first born son endured, to the physical ailments our second son Jeffery was afflicted with. Jeffery was born on August 26, 1971. Little did we know he would have to face the ugly disease of being a juvenile diabetic.

As his mother, I watched him in the hospital facing a disease that we were having to learn how to deal with. As the nurse came into the hospital room with that orange and a needle teaching him to give shots to himself, and at the same time telling us of the effect of the disease was overwhelming. Our son had to deal with it and it was a tool that the enemy has tried to use against him every since. You see the enemy does not like royal seed that will bring forth a harvest of souls for God's Kingdom.

Remember the Biblical account in 2 Kings 11:1-2, *"And when Athaliah the mother of Ahaziah saw that her son was dead, she arose and destroyed all the see royal.*

But Jehosheba, the daughter of king Joram, the son of Ahaziah, and stole him from among the king's sons which were slain; and they hid him, even him and his nurse, in the bedchamber from Athaliah, so that he was not slain."

The enemy wants only to destroy your royal seed whether it is a son, daughter, father, mother, brother or sister. When that baby is birthed in the natural realm or in your spiritual man the enemy will send a Athaliah to try and destroy the royal seed.

The enemy has no mercy and no desire to allow your Joash to come to the hour of his destiny. God will always have a Jehosheba standing in the wings to bring down the hand of the enemy through prayer and fasting, because he knows the importance of the birthing and sees the destiny God has placed on your life.

Not only did I face the devastation of a son that had been molested, and another with disease with no cure in sight at that time, I also endured a trauma in my marriage. Being tested by the fires is never easy, but it is for our growth and for a future that only God can see. I felt my heart had been crushed, brought to the very bottom and what would we do? Contrary to some people's opinion, we should have divorced, but you see, I made a vow when I married before God and man, that for better or worse, richer or poorer, sickness or health, until death do us part, we would remain together.

I remember the night when God took my broken heart and replaced it with a brand new heart. Were all the memories wiped away? No, No. But God has been faithful to bring us through all the fires.

In the midst of our trials, God always sends a ray of light into the darkness of the hour. Jeff has a great call on his life. He can sing, preach and has such an anointing to reach young people through the Spirit's direction.

You see, his life has been full of rejection by marriages, loneliness and depression. The enemy did not understand at the time what he was doing, but he was creating a miracle that would one day arise and destroy the very yoke from others, the same one he tried to tie around our son's neck.

Not one of our children has escaped the attack from the enemy since they were brought into the world, because they have a destiny God has designed for their lives. He will not let go, neither will I, and I know that God will not, for His plan will be perfected in the end.

Jeff has been attacked by the enemy since he was a child. He almost died one Wednesday night before going to Church. I had him in the emergency room earlier that day with what the doctor diagnosed as the flu. He gave Jeff some antibiotics and sent us home. Before the night came, Jeffery was drawing in his hands and feet and could not get his breath. He was dying right before our eyes, as once again the enemy tried to take another one of the precious seeds from us - but GOD.

When we arrived at the hospital and, after examining our son, a foreign doctor came out and asked my husband and I how long had our son been a diabetic. He was ten years old when he discovered the disease in our son's body. That night at the hospital his blood sugar count was over nine hundred. Yes, you read it right, nine hundred; the doctors looked at us and said it was a wonder he was not already in a coma or dead. (A miracle from the Father).

Through another trial, God proved Himself again to us. Our son is now thirty six years old and has dealt with bleeding in his eyes, two surgeries on both eyes and has lost sight in his left eye. We are standing in faith that God is still going to work a miracle in his body. Yes, He still does – MIRACLES ………………..

Jeff has two beautiful children: Lauren, which is our oldest grandchild, and her brother Corey. Many things has transpired in their lives, many heartaches, such devastations for small children to have to deal with, but I must say again God is a faithful God. He proves His love over again.

This book, "Through The Fires – God", is proof that you can come through whatever the enemy places in your way. God's Word declares in, Isaiah 54:17, *"No weapon that is formed against thee shall prosper; and every tongue that shall rise against thee in judgment thou shalt condemn. This is the heritage of the servants of the LORD, and their righteousness is of me, saith the LORD."*

I will write more concerning our son Jeff and his calling on his life and our oldest son Ken later. Both sons have distinct personalities, one loves the indoors, to listen to music, reading books and playing the piano while the other is an outdoors man. He loves the beauty of the woods and the things God has created, hunting, fishing, and singing. They are both beautiful gifts from God to me.

CHAPTER 2:

FAMILY

I sn't the journey strange God takes us on? Some days are filled with laughter while others are filled with pain, hurt and heartache. There are days when you feel you have lost *your song*, *your desire* and yes, even *the will to keep going on.*

Never did I know this journey would carry me and my family through death, into the court room and prison, but in the end it would bring out sweet fragrances in the midst of fiery trials.

Let's begin on June 12th 1977, on a Sunday morning at the Church where God's Spirit had been moving among the people. My mom had experienced such hurt and pain from my dad and his unmanageable anger; she was at a place she could not endure any more.

I loved my dad, but every time he would go into one of these uncontrollable rages of anger, you would not want to be in his way. (I remember the feeling of it as being picked up and thrown over onto the old red couch and landing with my back to it next to the fireplace.) Isn't it amazing how the enemy will take little foxes in our lives and turn them into demons, past and present?

On that Sunday morning my dad was overwhelmed with problems he could not handle and, instead of turning them over to God, he held on to them, but God's grace will always go to where we are, wooing us with His very special love.

The Spirit of the Lord was dealing with my dad, and God tried to reach him. That Sunday morning and night I found myself praying beside my dad, telling him how much I loved him. Little did I know this would be the last time I would get to see him alive.

Two or three days later, we received a phone call at home and my husband answered. The caller on the other end said to get to the hospital. The caller told my husband some of the details, but they were not shared with me. All I was told was my dad was sick and had been taken to the hospital. I knew it had to be serious, because my dad did not go to the doctor or hospital.

When we arrived at the hospital, I asked to see my mom. She was in one of the rooms of the hospital in such disillusionment. I asked her where dad was, but she could not respond, she was in shock. The nurse came in and I asked how he was doing and if I could see him.

She looked at us with her eyes and spoke with a coldness in her voice; it was clear she had been there many times before. Sheremarked, "don't you know that he is dead?"

Dead! My heart could not seem to understand what I was hearing with my ears. "Dead," how, when, what? You see, my youngest brother and dad had gotten into an argument and the demon of anger was manifested through my dad and he got out of control. My baby brother, only fifteen, had taken some drugs, was seeing a girl who's reputation was not the best, so my dad had told my brother he would not see her again. One thing led to another. My brother went to his room and my dad went out in the backyard and sat down on a culvert where they were doing some work. (My dad, after his anger got the best of him, would always begin to cry and vomit because of how far this spirit had taken him.)

My brother was in his room and a demon spirit spoke to him and said, "Take the gun off of the rack and go out and kill him." Being under the influence of the spirit of the enemy, which Jesus said in *John 10:10, "The thief cometh not, but for to steal, and to kill, and to destroy: I am come that they might have life, and that they might have it more abundantly."*

Do you understand who the enemy is? A thief (someone who comes to plunder, ravage), which comes to steal from us, (things that do not belong to him) to kill us, (mental, physically, spiritually,) and to utterly destroy (our hopes, dreams, and our destinies.) But Jesus said I have come, Praise God, *"to give life and give it more abundantly."*

My mom and our family were "tested in the fires." Our mom was so broken following the death of her husband and our father. Now her baby boy was on trial for his life. He was a very young teenager who had gotten lost somewhere along the way. I remember the days of the trial and all the pains we went through. Then the day came to hear the verdict.

The judge gave an order the courtroom that there would be no outburst. "Silence" he said, as the verdict is being read. Have you ever wondered how anyone can remain silent when you face the death of a loved one? The jury voted and my brother received life. My mom had trusted God in so many ways in her life, but that day changed her from being young to carrying the marks of pain and grief. My mom was only forty eight years old and, to carry on without dad, face the heartache of a son in prison, no ability to do anything else for him, and to see him every time on prison dates and leave had to be more than the natural man can bear, but with GOD. Her life was given to God, and through these trials, she would come out victorious.

Every Sunday, whether sick or well, she would go to the prison believing that my brother would one day be free from the prison bars of soul and body. You may be saying within your heart, he did not deserve to be free after taking the life of our father. You and I did not either, but God sent His Son to set us free. WE DID NOT DESERVE TO BE FREE, BUT GOD'S GRACE AND FORGIVENESS...............

Through the fiery trials my mom encountered, her Heavenly Father heard the earnest cry from the heart of a mother and answered. My brother got saved in prison and had such a transformation. His life with Christ was evident in his talk, walk and even in his face. He had made up his mind that whether he ever got free from the physical prison bars, he was free in his soul.

His life became such a testimony in prison and men began to watch his life. He gained favor as Joseph did in prison, and began to have prayer meetings, leading men which had been devastated by the thief, to the Savior and deliverer of their very souls.

God began giving him songs to write and sing; GOD WAS PREPARING HIM FOR HIS DESTINY the enemy had tried to delay for a long period of time. It was a little over eight years later that he walked out of prison a free man. He was called to preach the gospel and began to move in God's direction. Can you imagine the shame, guilt and overwhelming defeat other people will put on you when they see you? You have enough to deal with and don't need anything piled on.

We should look into the eyes of God and see what our gracious Father has done. You see, I had that unforgiving spirit and anger that came upon me when I would see my brother. I asked God to help me and let me see the love God had put in my brother.

What you do not deal with today will come back to defeat you tomorrow. You cannot carry unforgiveness and live in the fullness of your walk with God. No matter what has happened in your life, you must forgive and be made whole. Thank God, I did let go of it all and we have a sweet fellowship.

My brother has become one of the greatest preachers, song writers and is a great brother. (His story is yet to be told). He has written many powerful songs under the sweet anointing of the Father). He was such a very special baby when mom brought him home from the hospital. I helped take care of him as he grew up because I was the oldest of five children. He was a pure joy to take care of while mom helped dad to make a living.

Our dad was buried on June 30th 1977. It is almost unbelievable when you think how fast the years have passed. He was fifty two when he died, and I think of all the things he could have seen happen in his family if he had lived.

He has two sons that are ministers of the Gospel, my sister Vickey, who is a mighty prayer warrior, and me, his daughter, who is also a minister of the Gospel. There are also grandchildren who are coming up that have destiny written all over their lives.

Dad, we love you and look forward to seeing you again when we reunite as a family together in heaven.

My mom was to yet experience another terrible trial in her life concerning my oldest sister. When she was still at home with my mom and dad, Shelby, who was sixteen, insisted on marrying a man that was twenty seven years old. My father could not seem to agree with them. They were either to be allowed to get married or they would run off. My dad finally gave in and my sister and her husband left and moved to South Carolina. My sister was sixteen with blond hair and was a beautiful young person, very naive, lonely for attention and love, just wanting to get away from home and things she saw.

Her life became a tangled web of marriages, alcohol, some drugs, and many affairs and many more marriages. Nothing seemed to satisfy her. You see, she was looking for the answers in all the wrong places and people. Only true peace can be found in Jesus Christ. Shelby had been brought up in the Church and knew the Spirit of the Lord and also a praying mother. YOU CANNOT GET AWAY, NO MATTER HOW FAR YOU RUN…….. (Sometimes the glitter and sounds of this world will draw you in until you are completely lost in it, and can't remember how to get home to God). There must always be someone standing in the gap for your loved ones, to defeat the enemy through intense warfare, then victory comes.

Just two weeks before Christmas, we had been praying that God would save her and bring her home. She always felt as if she was the black sheep of the family, but we loved her and never made her feel unloved in any way.

My husband and I were at the mall shopping for last minute Christmas when my two brothers came to find us. They had some very sad news, and nothing would prepare me for what I was about to hear from them.

I began to think immediately that something must be wrong with mom because she had been sick, but that was not the fiery trial we would have to go through this time. My brothers looked at me and said "we have some bad news. Shelby has just died from a massive heart attack at the age of thirty six."

Once again, our family was being tested by the fires. Shelby had called two weeks before Christmas and said to me she was tired of the life she had been living and wanted to give it all to God. I began to pray for her and she surrendered everything to Him. She was in South Carolina and I was in Statesboro. You see, there is no distance with the God we serve; He is able to save to the uttermost.

The enemy, the accuser of the brethren, began to say to me that she had not truly received the Lord and she was in hell. He loves to taunt the children of God in their minds, and even after the seed has been planted and growth has taken place, the Devil will still try to snatch away the victory from our minds. The Word of God declares in 1 John 4:4, *"Ye are of God, little children, and have overcome them: because greater is he that is in you, than he that is in the world."*

I said to the Lord "when get to South Carolina where her body is, please let me know everything is alright and give me the peace of mind I need." When we walked up to the coffin and looked, there was a smile on her face that the mortician could not wipe off.

Talking about peace that passes all understanding, it came that day for mom and all the family. I had come through the death of a child, father, a sister, and only six years later would lose my mother to death. Many losses have come to me, and it will seem strange to some, but every loss has made me stronger and I have endured in the face of the enemy.

My mother's death is a victory that you don't want to forget. Her crying, sacrifices, love, and dedication to our father, and to her children, was about to give her the sweetest victory over the enemy.

I remember she had been very ill for a long time. Most of her large intestines had been removed, and she was in and out of the hospital over and over, still battling with the disease of diverticulitis. She was placed in St. Joseph's Hospital in Savannah, Georgia, where many tests were run. The doctor then came to talk with us about what they had found. X-rays had shown a dark spot on her small intestine; they would take her down and operate, remove the infected area and then come back to speak with us.

They took her out of the Intensive Care room into the operating room where the doctors were waiting to remove the infected part of the small intestine. It was only after about 45 minutes later when they called for the family to come into the waiting room. Who can prepare you what you are about to hear, except God? The doctor sat down and told us that our mom would die that night or the next morning. Gangrene had already invaded her body. Her temperature was raging up to 106 and she did not know any of us. Our hearts were breaking to know that we only had a few hours with her. Another loss in our family caused us to gather even closer together as we understood this was our mother, and heaven was about to gain another angel.

I walked into the room where she was and began to ask her if she knew who I was. She blinked her eyes, and in the natural, she would not have recognized me, but the Lord allowed her to understand who I was. Guilt had tried to invade my mind because I was gone from home in revivals most of the time she was sick.

I was in a three-week revival in Cairo where many people were being saved and God was doing glorious works in our midst. When the pastor received the phone call at the parsonage, asking to speak with me, I thought mom was sicker than she had been before, but that she would get better and go home. God will always prepare us for what is about to happen in our lives. I shared with her how much I loved her and thanked her for her faithfulness to God, then our father and and for remaining with him when others would have walked away, and then for taking care of us and praying over us.

I began to sing the old songs of Zion that had taken her through those long dark trials and brought her total victory. The Spirit led me to read Revelation 21 to her and remind her that in 1 Corinthians 2:9, the Word declares, *"But as it is written, Eye hath not seen nor ear heard, neither have entered into the heart of man, the things which GOD hath prepared for them that love him."*

I reminded her the same Sweet Holy Ghost that was with her through the death of dad, my sister Shelby, and in the court room when the verdict was read for my brother to go to prison, was in the room and He would take her hand and that she would have no fear. I was privileged to watch the precious home going of mom as she shook off the remains of this old earth and all of its cares, as death entered the room.

My mom was blind in her left eye and had not been able to see anything out of it, but when the presence of the Lord entered the room, and took her by the hand to cross over, she said, "Well, Praise the Lord", looked up and said, "Lord." She was ushered into the presence of the King of Glory on October 12, 1996, six years after my sister's death.

There, I believe, was a reunion with my sister and my dad, but most of all Jesus Christ who had carried her through all the fires. She had found Him faithful and would rest from all of her labors; being in His Presence, she was now able to understand it was worth it all.

The old hymn we often sang in Church as a small girl, even now into my senior years, proved true to mom and all the other saints who have gone on. It will also become reality for you and me one day. And it says, "It will be worth it all when we see Jesus, all sorrows will be gone, when we see Christ, One glimpse of His dear face all sorrows will erase, and gladly run this race till we will see Christ."

Enjoy your rest and peace, Mom. We love and miss you dearly, but we know we shall see you again.

She had a victorious encounter with the King, who had brought her through the dark nights, loneliness, pain and heartache. She found Him as true as His precious Word, Isaiah 43:2-3a, *"When thou passest through the waters, I will be with thee; and through the rivers, they shall not overflow thee: when thou walkest through the fire, thou shalt not be burned; neither shall the flame kindle upon thee. For I am the LORD thy God, the Holy One of Israel, thy Savior."*

My oldest brother has gone through his own hot fiery trials but came out with victory. He is a Pastor and great administrator; he was Pastor of several different Churches and carried them into new levels through the Word of God. He also has been given a gift of building, a gift my dad also had.

My brother has built several new sanctuaries and family life centers, and every detail in so unique, accurate and beautiful. My brother believes in the old saying, as I do, and those gone on before us, "if you are going do anything it is worth doing it right." As the oldest son of the family he has dealt with the loss of dad in a different way than we did.

Most boys miss the opportunity of fishing, (which my dad loved to do) hunting and just being able to be around him. Questions I am sure that he would love to be able to sit and talk with him concerning. There is always a loss within a family with mom and dad both gone. There are empty feelings inside your home and heart at holidays, family reunions, or at their birthdays, and only God Himself can fill the void and longing that is inside to see, touch and just feel them around you.

My dad died on June 30, 1977 at the age of fifty two, when people are really just beginning to live their lives and enjoy children, grandchildren and great grandchildren. My sister passed away on December 24, 1990 at the age of thirty six, and mom passed away on October 12, 1996 at the age of sixty seven.

These were great losses for our family, but I must express again, only God can carry you through the trials of life; you can still have sweet peace and victory abiding within. After all, what a great reunion we will have when we get home. They are waiting together, enjoying all the Father has in His house and we will one day join with them.

Last, but not least, is my youngest sister. She also, like all of us, has faced trials of difficulties. She is not a preacher that stands in a pulpit and proclaims the Gospel, but she is the force behind those of us who do. There have been many days and nights she has spent in prayer and fasting for my two brothers and me.

She has stayed on her knees in tears and as we used to hear the old saints say, she stayed there until she had prayed through for herself, and us ministers fighting on the front lines. She would pray for her family, pastor and friends who would call her up and share things with her to pray about, and she would. God would send the answers to help them on their journey to reach their destiny because of my sister's dedication in prayer.

Oftentimes we forget those who are in the background, and seem to forget that they are so needful. As Charles Finney said, "their prayers help me to be able to do what I do."

My sister dealt with depression after my mom passed away because she was with her more than me. She felt the intense loneliness of her not being there, to go shopping, eating lunch and just being around to talk with. They were very close in their relationship, and my sister felt the overwhelming pressure of picking up and going on.

She tried to take her life on three different occasions because of issues from the past and the death of mom. The demons we try to hide from others keep coming up to taunt, and they literally try to destroy us. Mom had prayed and sought God for her. Prayers of the saints just keep persevering and holding us strong in the hands of God. The Word of God is alive forever and declares in Isaiah 54:17, *"No weapon that is formed against thee shall prosper; and every tongue that shall rise against thee in judgment thou shalt condemn. This is the heritage of the servants of the LORD, and their righteousness is of me, saith the LORD."*

I have said many times to people that if you were to look and judge the Kearney family by what you see and have heard, you would probably think they were not worth wasting your time on. When men look through the eyes of the natural, all they see is brokenness, confusion and unworthiness to be helped. But, Praise the Lord, when He looks at us He still sees something beautiful and will shape us by His mighty Hands into vessels of honor, and He will take us to our destiny.

Jeremiah 18:1-4 declares, *"The word which came to Jeremiah from the LORD, saying, arise, and go down to the potter's house, and there I will cause thee to hear my words. Then I went down to the potter's house, and, behold, he wrought a work on the wheels. And the vessel that he made of clay was marred in the hand of the potter; so he made it again another vessel, as seemed good to the potter to make it."*

Even now as you read this book, you may think your life is not worth anything and you have too many real demons you battle with, or broken things, and, after all, who could mend all of these things? The answer that has brought me thus far and will continue to carry me is not religion, wealth, or good morals. It is a relationship with Him; His name is Jesus, Savior, Deliverer, Friend, Father, Brother, one that is never changing and meets you at your point of brokenness.

May I suggest to you before we continue on this journey that you surrender everything at the foot of the Cross?

Jesus gave us a wonderful invitation in His Word in Matthew 11:28, *"Come unto me, all ye that labor and are heavy laden, and I will give you rest."* WHY NOT ACCEPT IT TODAY AND BE FREE? Will you pray with me right now this prayer? It is your choice, you can be free.

"Heavenly Father, Please forgive me and come into my life as my Savior. I understand that your love will heal me of all my pain, heartache and brokenness and give me a peace past my understanding and fill my life with your joy. I also give you the person or persons who have damaged my life and caused me grief. I surrender my will to you today and thank you for saving, healing and bringing restoration completely. Amen."

CHAPTER 3:

OUR EARLY BEGINNINGS

My husband and I were entering into our eighth year of marriage when we received the great news that our third child was on the way. In my times before God, I would always thank Him for my two sons and the joy they brought to me. Kenny was seven and Jeffery was five and half years old, and I had such a desire to have a daughter. On March 18th, 1975, our girl was born. A daughter is someone, whom we as mothers, will dress up in frills and lace, have some of the greatest tea parties together and then, as she becomes older, is someone you can share secrets with and listen to the dreams she has.

My children are gifts from God and when each one entered into this world, I laid my hands on them and blessed them. I asked God to give them gifts, talents and abilities, and whatever plan He had for them would be a joy to Him and to us as their parents.

I have watched as God has put His Hands on their lives and given them the ability to sing, to play instruments and write songs. I also called them forth to become an Evangelist, Pastor, Teacher, Pastors' Wife, or to become one of the best lay persons in the congregation of a local church, and to pray for their Church and Pastor.

Our daughter is now grown, married and has three children of her own, two boys and a girl. She is the best mom and wife and loves the Lord and has a definite destiny on her life. She is a very anointed singer with a destiny for greater and greater things in the anointing. I believe if she will begin to step up into her calling she will lead other women into the realm of the supernatural. It is amazing to watch my three children who have their own unique personalities and gifting. On the other side of that is to watch your children as they shun the God-given call and begin to take journeys into the far country as the prodigal son did.

My best days are ahead, I believe, as I watch them come forth with God and tear down strongholds of the enemy over their lives and the lives of the people that have struggled with the same issues. We were not put here just to occupy space and time, but to be productive in the Kingdom of God. There are lessons we go through on this journey that we must learn. We will either learn them the first time or we will continue to go around and around again, until we get it.

WHY? Because God has placed people in our lives that may be going through or who are entering a time of testing, and we will be there to tell them God will do it for them also. Our testimonies will become lights in the valleys of their lives.

You may be asking how can I help anyone when I have so many questions that seem to keep surrounding me. It feels as if you are being smothered by the circumstances, and if there is a spark of hope, the enemy will see to it that you do not see any light at the end of tunnel, but only darkness.

We are not the first individuals who questioned where are you, God. In the Old Testament, the story is told of Elijah the prophet sent from God with destiny written all over his life. He was sent to preach against the wicked King Ahab, his wife Jezebel and the idolatry they had set up in the land.

The story is related in 1 Kings 19. Understand, here is a man with a calling from God, divine direction and and as I said, destiny written on his heart and life. He was only human and he asked this question: "God, have you left me alone in this? Why have you not answered me? Do you not care about me and all that I am facing? Do you not see the pressure the enemy is putting on me?"

The answer to all those questions is YES. The Word of God declares in Jeremiah 29:11, *"For I know the thoughts that I think toward you, saith the LORD, thoughts of peace, and not of evil, to give you an expected end.* God had a destiny for each of their lives, and also for us. We see Elijah, Moses, Abraham, Job, David, Esther and all the other great men and women in the Bible. It was the deserts of their lives and ours that brings us to maturity and gives us a great expected end.

Do not be surprised that the enemy will come with his crafty devices to try and distract you from your destiny. He is plotting your downfall if you are a threat to his kingdom of darkness.

The Spirit spoke to my heart recently and said, *"Deserts will come into your life but there will always be the "Rose of Sharon," to meet you and give you the fragrance of His anointing to carry you through."* As a young couple, we went through times of deserts of sicknesses, financial woes, and marriage problems, but God has always helped us.

Allow me to share with you several personal illustrations of how God came to me during sickness in my body. My husband was a professional meat cutter by trade for 27 years. He had worked in this area since being discharged from service in the U.S. Army in November 1968.

Years later we purchased and operated a business where we slaughtered and processed hogs and cows. I had gotten sick during that time and was back and forth to the doctors trying to find out what the problem was. I was not able to eat, lost weight and became so weak until I was bedridden.

The doctors diagnosed the problem as diverticulitis; the same problem my mom had, I now had. We were having prayer meetings in the homes of different ladies on Tuesday morning each week. I was so desirous to be there because I knew God would show up and do great things.

The ladies of the prayer meeting knew I had been sick and as they began to pray, and the Spirit directed them to come get me and take me back to the prayer meeting. Out of the bed of sickness I came, and as the women of faith prayed and circled around, God came and healed me.

As I said, I had not been able to eat and keep anything in my system, but I knew my Father had reached down His mighty hand and healed my body. I came back from the prayer meeting, went over to the business we owned and told my husband the good news. I told him I wanted to go to town and get the biggest McDonald's hamburger and fries to eat. Praise the Lord, He is a healing Jesus. That is one of many times when God came to where I was and healed me.

In 2001 I was diagnosed with high blood pressure; I would get out of the bed in the morning and it would be 198/95. I was taking blood pressure medicine and become so tired and sluggish. One night in a revival, God instantly healed me of the condition and I have not taken any more medication. My blood pressure is normal and I am praising my Lord for healing power.

My story would never end if I told you of the healings God has done in my life, <u>physically</u>, <u>emotionally</u>, and <u>spiritually</u>.

He is *El-Shaddai*, *"the God that is more than enough."*

Our oldest son literally had a miracle in his life when he was only nine. He had started wearing glasses when he was 5. The doctor who examined his eyes stated he had the same problem I have with my eyes. His little glasses were as thick as the bottom of a Coca-Cola bottle. The doctor said he would always have to wear glasses, but God always has the last word.

We had started a revival at our home Church with Dr. T. L. Lowery preaching. On a Sunday morning my husband was one of the ushers and a man whom we had never seen before or since (we believe he was a angel), told my husband he had been praying for him the whole service. My husband considered that very strange since we did not know him, and that he would be concerned to pray for our son. The Word of God says in Hebrews 13:2, *"Be not forgetful to entertain strangers; for thereby some have entertained angels unawares."* My husband and I encouraged our son to go down for prayer, and he did.

Child-like faith is all we need in order to receive our miracle from God. We went home from the service that morning. Our son did not tell us, but he went outside, took a hammer and smashed his glasses. A day or two later his father saw him reading (he would always experience headaches) without his glasses and asked him where they were. He looked up at his dad and said, "I broke them up, God healed me." From that day forward he never wore glasses again.

Many days were still ahead that would try our faith in God, but He always proved to be faithful. Through times of financial troubles in our business, when the interest rate skyrocketed and people no longer slaughtered cows and hogs as they had done in the past, our business went down.

There is a principal we have lived by in Malachi 2:10, *"Bring ye all the tithes into the storehouse, that there may be meat in mine house, and prove me now herewith, saith the LORD of hosts, if I will not open you the windows of heaven, and pour you out a blessing, that there shall not be room enough to receive it."*

My husband and I have been a part of this promise since we got married. Even before then as a young girl babysitting or doing odd jobs, I believed the promise. No one forced us, it was our privilege to do so in honor of God's Word in our lives. We pay the 10th of our income in tithe and gave our offerings.

Because we were obedient to God's Word, he brought victory to us and met every need we have had. I did not say our desires were always met, but our needs were. We owed a light bill in our business which was $628.00, and it was due the next day. This was on a Wednesday and we had church that night and only had $5.00 left. We had not shared our need with anyone, but I had taken it to the Lord.

That night when we got to Church, the pastor said he had been burdened for a couple in the Church and the Lord spoke to him to receive an offering that night. There were only about 30-35 people in the service that night. He did not say who the couple was, so my husband and I looked at each other and gave the last $5.00 we had.

After the service the pastor came up to us and said that God has spoken to him that we had a need. He handed us the offering and it was $633.00, enough to pay the light bill and our $5.00 came back. God is a faithful Father.

The Word declares that He is *Jehovah-Jireh*, *"the Lord that provides."* No matter what it is that you need He is your provider.

It takes no faith at all to trust God when everything is at your disposal, you have money in the bank, food in the pantry, children and family are all well, but it is quite different when you have nothing.

I will share one more story with you about how God has met our needs. We were living in a home on Debbie Drive in Statesboro, and we had struggled financially as a young couple. We had very little food in the house, not really enough to fix a complete meal.

I had been praying during the day and the Lord sent a servant from God who began knocking on my door. I opened the door and she said that God had sent her by to pray over my cabinets. I started crying and while she was praying, the Holy Ghost spoke to me and said, "from this day forward your cabinets will never be bare." You may ask the question have they? No!!! God has taken care of it all, the cabinets have always had food and more.

I share these stories with you because they are faith builders to me that GOD IS MORE THAN SUFFICENT TO TAKE CARE OF YOU AND ME AND STILL MORE THAN ENOUGH.

Aren't we so much like the children of Israel? While God is in our midst and all is calm we rest, but as soon as something doesn't go as we think it should, we begin to question the ability of God. Look in Psalm 78:19, *"Yea, they spake against God; they said, Can God furnish a table in the wilderness?"*

Can you imagine the heart of God? He has created us in His image, supplied every need we have and when one issue comes where we don't see the answer, we question whether He is big enough, and does He qualify?

Can God furnish a table in the wilderness? Let me remind you what He did for the children of Israel. He tells them Psalm 78:

> Verse 12, *"Marvelous things did he in the sight of their fathers, in the land of Egypt, in the field of Zoan.*
>
> V. 13, *"He divided the red sea, and caused them to pass through; and He made the waters to stand as an heap.* (The miracle of the Red Sea crossing).
>
> V.14, *"In the daytime also He led them with a cloud, and all the night with a light of fire.*
>
> V.15, *"He clave the rocks in the wilderness, and gave them drink as out of the great depths.* (the water out of the rock)
>
> V.16, *"He brought streams also out of the rock, and caused waters to run down like rivers* (this means that this was no slight trickle that came out of the rock, but rather a small river – – – enough to quench the thirst of some three million people, plus all of the animals.)

Can God furnish a table in the wilderness? HE COULD AND HE DID!

God help us not doubt you in the midst of our wilderness.

As I was preparing myself to come before the people in revival and deliver the Word of God, He spoke this to me, *"IF YOU WILL, I WILL"*. If you will obey my Word, then I will fulfill it................

In other words, unbelief will cancel out your blessings. Hebrews 11:6 declares, *"But without faith It is impossible to please him: for he that cometh to God must believe that*

He is, and that He is a rewarder of them that diligently seek Him."

I have shared just a small portion of what God has done in our lives. Oh, the enemy has said many times, "God does not care about you and your situation, if He did He would have already answered."

But, you see, God is not on our time table. It may appear He is four days late, but He is on time. Do not be discouraged, because God is trustworthy, faithful and ever present to help us.

CHAPTER 4:

MENTORS OF MY LIFE

The he dictionary defines <u>mentor</u> as _"a wise and trusted counselor or teacher."_ As I write this book, my definition of mentor is someone who sees destiny in your life and is willing to spend and be spent for the cause of Christ in your life in order to help you accomplish the greatness, never receiving the applause for themselves.

A mentor is most definitely a _<u>wise person,</u>_ maybe not through the eyes of the world by intellect, educational background or even worldly wisdom, but is a person who gives you instruction from and with God. Men cannot give this wisdom in the natural.

A mentor is also a _<u>trusted counselor.</u>_ Whatever you need to tell them it is kept in confidence and only shared to the Father through prayer.

A mentor is a _<u>teacher.</u>_ Mentors do not teach by words only, but by their very spirit of meekness, kindness and most, of all, just living the same day in and out. The Pentecostal people call it, " walking the walk and talking the talk. They do not say, "Do as I tell you, but follow me as I follow Christ."

It seems to me that we have heard those words before from the great Apostle Paul in 1 Corinthians 11:1, _"Be_ *ye followers (imitators) of me, even as I also am of Christ.* (Those who imitate Christ have a right to call upon others to imitate them.) Paul also said in Philippians 3:17, *"Brethren, be followers together of me, and mark them which walk so as ye have us for an example."* (observe intently) Paul had mentors in his life: Barnabas, John Mark and individuals in the churches where he ministered. He took the time to be wise, trusted, and a great teacher.

Where would we be without mentors in our lives? I am sure I would not be where I am today.

This chapter in my life in one of the most vital, because men and women forgot about their everyday troubles, their tiredness on Tuesday and Thursday nights in order to teach me the principles of God's Word, and living it before me.

There were women of God who forgot they had children of their own and took me under their loving care and instructed, cried and laughed with me. They taught me about Him and the greatness of our God.

These men and women of God lived out their lives before me and showed me the way to the throne in times of distress, joy and hopelessness.

I dedicate to them the precious legacy they left behind for me, so that I may become all that God would have me be. In turn, that I will help mentor other people to reach their full potential and destiny in God.

There is no success without sacrifice. Understand that in my life time I had a lot of heroes in the faith, but few mentors. May I share with you just a two or three that impacted my life and the lives of others who were blessed to be around them?

Brother Dudley Bradley, Sr., my Sunday school teacher, had been paralyzed from the neck down in a swimming accident. He was a dedicated Christian who lived for Christ and loved us young people. He would teach us the Word of God and, most importantly, he would live out his Christian walk.

I was privileged later in my young adult life to work with him in his accounting firm as his secretary and other positions in the office for 9 ½ years. He was always the Christian gentleman he had been as our teacher. Thank God he put into my life, through prayer, examples and dedication, what God can do through the most difficult days of your life. If anyone can understand that, it would be Brother Dudley Bradley as he battled through the fires of life and had been victorious.

Then there was Sister Edna Hood, a little petite lady in the Church in Statesboro, along with her husband Brother Gordon Hood. Sister Hood had such a faith in her God that it did not matter what she was facing, you would only see joy on her face.

I have walked into the church many times as a young teenager, and later becoming a wife and mother, to hear Sister Hood say as she hugged our necks, "God loves you and I do, too. I have been praying for you this week." With that beautiful smile and little chuckle in her laughter, you knew your life was going to be alright.

She would shout under such an anointing and raise her little hand and say, "Ooo, thank you Jesus." She died the same as she lived. Later on in life, when her mind was taken from her by the disease called Alzheimer's, she could not even recognize her own family, but she knew who God was. One day when he was off from work, my husband went to visit with her. He spoke of the pastor by name and the church and she would just begin to hum. My husband then proceeded to say to her, "you love the Lord don't you, Sister Hood?" Sister Hood would begin to speak in tongues and be caught up in His presence.

The lady that was sitting with her said to my husband, "now she loves that Holy Ghost." You see, in dying, you can still be a great teacher, YOU CAN SHOW SOMEONE HOW TO DIE IN THE ARMS OF JESUS.........

Last, but not least, is Sister Reather Martin. Sister Martin came to a personal relationship with the Lord after many tragedies in her life. She was like Saul, which later became the Apostle Paul; she had a Damascus Road experience. Everyone she knew soon understood this was not the same woman they had known before. Sister Martin had seven children of her own, three sons and four daughters.

Sister Martin seemed to understand the very times in my mom's life, and ours as children, that we needed to go home with her on Sunday. She would take us home and mentor us through her love and dedication.

When Sunday dinner was ready, she would call us from the yard where we had been playing and we would sit down to eat fried chicken, dumplings, macaroni and cheese, homemade biscuits and some kind of dessert. After we ate, she would call us in to pray over us and we would lay down and rest so that we would be ready for Church that night.

Her loving arms and big hands would wrap around you and she would pray for you and God would always touch. She left her mark where she went and whatever she touched. Thank God she left her mark on me through the anointing she had. Sister Martin is the one that came to my house and prayed over my cabinets.

She became my second mom. She and my mom became great friends after dad's death. They would go places together to eat and share about the love of God. Sister Martin was like my mom in many ways. She had encountered children who had been away from God, she had a husband that was not saved and she dealt with pain and brokenness in her own life. Sister Martin, like mom, had faced many days of sickness where she had only one kidney. Sister Martin's faith would bring her through her own fiery trials, and she would see victory time and time again.

All the great fun times, wonderful home cooked meals, and just being with her is nothing to compare the to the legacy of prayer she left me. Any time there was a need, she would gather her girls around her and they would have prayer meeting right there in their home.

Money cannot buy the priceless gift of prayer and the rewards of seeking Him and knowing that He will answer you. Sister Martin is a mentor time will not be able to erase from me in my life.

Any time she or her family had a problem, it was taken to the problem solver. That was her way of life; she knew Him.

Sister Martin has now gone to heaven where I believe her faithfulness has paid off. She has left a legacy of prayer that continues even after her death. She made an impact on people's lives, along with leaders she saw in the Spirit, and they have arisen to carry on her vision.

Last, but surely not least, was my mom. I watched her when she was so tired, tested and pulled from every direction but, her faith in God kept her standing. She taught me that no matter how difficult your circumstances or surroundings, you can make it with Him by your side.

I would not be able to tell you of all the mentors in my life, but here are a few that left nuggets for me to gleam from. Some were diamonds, I would later understand that in life's journey.

1. <u>Brother Waters:</u> He was poor, had no real education, but he knew how to honor the servants of God. He would never fail to set a glass of water on

the pulpit for those who labored before the Lord. Jesus said in Matthew 25:21, *"Well done, thou good and faithful servant: thou hast been faithful over a few things. I will make thee ruler over many things, enter thou into the joy of thy Lord."*

2. <u>Brother Albert & Sister Billie Murray</u>: They took me into their home and trusted me to keep their children. The Murray's were always pouring prayer and encouraging words into my life that would carry me on into my destiny. She prepared my veil for my wedding, took care of taking the pictures and helped with the reception.

3. <u>Reverend Elmer Golden, Jr</u>: He was the pastor who came with a vision to move us from where we were in the Church. We had been stagnated in many areas of our lives, but a man of God helped to show what to do in order to move into new lands and claim the promise of God. A man of God that lived out his convictions, stood in the gap as a moral leader in the community against pornography and alcohol. Everywhere he went, people knew him for the man of God he was. Is that not what a true leader and mentor is all about? Living out your life before the people that they may follow the pattern of Godly leadership. He stood beside my mom and us through the death of my father, in the court room as our hearts were breaking when the verdict was read. He remained a constant strength in those days and continues on to be the man of God he has always been. We love you dearly, Pastor, Friend.

Often, when life gives us gems to treasure, we seem to forget how really precious they were. Too many times we have taken their mentoring for granted, but I want to say. THANK YOU, THANK YOU.

In his book "Developing The Leaders Around You", John Maxwell writes on page 69, "When you believe in people, you motivate them and release their potential. And people can sense intuitively when a person really believes in them. Anyone can see people as they are. It takes a leader to see what they can become, encourage them to grow in that direction, and believe that they will do it."

Some of these men and women probably never saw themselves as real leaders, but they were.

Investing into others always takes something from us. All the benefits of giving returns when we see the greatness we have helped develop in them, because we saw their destiny and helped to further the Kingdom of God through the eyes of God.

CHAPTER 5:

EVANGELIST

As you are reading through this book, you should understand my life has been one tragedy after another, but it has built *character*, *faith* and *maturity* in me I needed in order to fulfill the destiny God put within me.

Were it not for the fiery trials I encountered, I would not be able to tell you no matter what you face in your life, or what life gives you to endure, you can make with Him.

From the beginning, in the womb of my mother, the Lord knew me. The devil and his demons have tried to stop, destroy and break me under the load of it all, but praise the Lord, I have won!

In the early days of my life, after the Lord had saved me, sanctified and filled me with the wonderful Holy Ghost, I knew God had a plan for me. As a teenager in the Church, God used me to be part of the youth choir. We went to churches on the district and had revivals.

The Lord would anoint us to bless people as the Spirit would come down. As I got older in the Church, I was was used in the nursery to help take care of the children. Often times people get disgruntled because they are asked to work in the nursery. Who knows what mother may come into our Church and get saved from the abusive situation in her marriage and healing from sexual encounters; and to think that we were part of that by being willing to help in the nursery. What a great opportunity to pray over the babies, to anoint them for their lives and pray protection over their minds.

Men and women began to recognize that God had his hand on me; after I was married I taught Sunday school from the nursery all the way up to the teenager's class. Later, I had the privilege of teaching the adult class where His Spirit was so greatly manifested.

After serving the Church in different areas, I was elected as President of the Ladies Ministries. God was preparing me for the future He had planned for me.

Sometimes we wonder, "why I am working in the kitchen, cleaning the bathrooms, working in the yards to keep the outside of God's House beautiful?" Well, I will give you the answer to that. We cannot become leaders until we become servants.

The prime example of being that servant is our Heavenly Father when He took a towel and washed the feet of Peter. We must learn humility before we become great leaders ourselves.

I was a very reserved and shy person in school. I would not even get up in front of the class to give book reports. My inadequate feelings, my low self-esteem, and overwhelming desire to be accepted left me devastated.

Men can never fill the emptiness and void in your life; the only one who can do that is our Heavenly Father. He *"loves us with an everlasting love."* We are His creation, made in the likeness of Him.

God began to use me in the deeper ways of His Spirit. I had learned to know His voice and obey Him. When we were still at the business we owned, our children were in a Christian school, and I would take them there in the morning and in the afternoon go back and get them.

We lived about fourteen miles outside of Statesboro, and I had left that day to pick them up. When I got to the school the Spirit spoke to me not to go back the way I came. I was arguing with God, as we so often do, in order for things to get accomplished, or when we are tired and just want to do it our way. After all, we know more than He does..

The Spirit spoke again, and the third time, I turned in the opposite direction and stopped, as the Spirit directed me to go inside a produce business. I took the children out of the car, went inside and it began to rain, hail was falling and the wind was uncontrollable. I had not heard any weather reports about what was happening, even at that very hour.

Later, I understood in the Spirit that it was alright for me to leave. When we left the produce business and got outside the city limits to a store on the hill, I saw trees uprooted, and the path straight where I would have gone was torn out.

When I reached the store on the hill, I got out to call my husband to let him know we were delayed by the weather, and then I understood the telephone lines were down. The owner of the store said to me, "It is good that you were not here any sooner, you would have gotten caught up in the path of the tornado" that has just come through the very direction I usually traveled to get back home. The tornado ripped through Statesboro leaving a subdivision in shambles, and a brand new funeral home leveled to the ground. Many homes and businesses were completely destroyed.

If we as His children can have listening ears, we will avoid a lot of pitfalls in our lives. He is the Creator, our

Father. The Word declares in Matthew 10:30, *"But the very hairs of your head are all numbered."*

HE CAN BE TRUSTED!!!!!

At the place where our business was, I had gotten caught up in a pity party concerning what I did not have instead of being thankful for what He had blessed me with.

I would usually get up on Saturday when the business was closed and go to town to window shop. I wanted a new dress, shoes or other things like other people had. They would come to church with a new this or that. I would get overwhelmed and the enemy would use that to keep me from listening and hearing the voice of God for direction.

Satan does not care what it is he uses against you, big or small. *IT IS A DISTRACTION REGARDLESS..............* Remember why? To keep you from your destiny.

I began to weep and ask God to forgive me and help me know what He had planned for me. That day was a gift from Him, just like every day. We forget to stop and smell the fragrance of the flowers in bloom, hear the singing of the birds, to see the beauty of His creation all around us. That is Satan's plan. Get distracted on yourself and your needs, and forget about everyone else.

Praise the Lord! I did have listening ears to the Spirit as He began to speak. He sent me that day to three different individuals and families. I was supposed to carry a bottle of oil with me to anoint and pray with them.

When I got to the first house to pray for my brother-in-law, who had been down in the bed for a week unable to go to work, the Spirit came upon me. I laid hands on him and he was healed. He began to praise the Lord and later got out of the bed, went to the Church that night and went back to work with healing and a smile on his face.

The second place the Spirit spoke to me to go to was a friend's house to pray over the two daughters. I did not know where they were, but when the door opened, their mother understood it was a divine appointment. I went straight down the hall, found the two girls in their room and began to pray over them. I do not know all that God did, but it was a turn around in the Spirit, and salvation for another. Later in life we would share what the Lord had done for them as they became women of God with families of their own.

The third assignment from God was for one of the sisters in the Church, whose name was Carolyn. The Spirit directed me to go to her house and pray over her. I obeyed and left. On Monday afternoon I received a phone call, and the sister said to me, "I know why you came to my house Saturday and prayed for me."

She worked in Savannah, and on her way home it began to storm and she could hardly see in front of her. She realized a transfer truck was just behind her. All of a sudden, the car hit a water spot in the road, and her car ended up going into the ditch, bouncing back up on the road, and when she looked, the truck was nowhere to be seen and her life was spared.

God does have direction for our lives if we will be sensitive to His voice. I learned valuable lessons that would later become relevant to my calling from God.

The *gift of knowledge and prophecy* was being used in my life as I prayed with people in the altars and at prayer meetings. Little did I know that would become part of the destiny in my life.

My calling from God came on May 8th 1989. We were in a Holy Ghost revival with such an anointing flowing every night in the services. God was working through the servant he sent to us.

During that revival, we saw manifestations of the Holy Ghost as He spoke things to the church, to individuals and the very atmosphere was charged with His presence.

God had been using me in the altars to pray with people and it was such an awesome blessing from Him. At the end of the service, the man of God looked at me and said, "Sister please come and let me pray for you."

I immediately went up and God began to give forth a word over me. The Lord said that I did not understand what was about to happen to me, but He was going to doing something great.

I was slain in the Spirit, and the Holy Ghost spoke these words to me, which I will never forget. He said, "my daughter, I have called you to preach my Word. Don't look to the right or left, keep your eyes on Me. The enemy will be behind you and I will go before you. I have anointed you; many souls will be saved and delivered. Go in my name and I will do it."

I was helped up off the floor by my husband and I was so under the influence of the Spirit until I was drunk. *Ephesians 5:18, " And be not drunk with wine (speaks of being controlled by alcoholic beverage, which Paul desires to use as an example), wherein is excess; but be filled with the Spirit) being controlled by the Spirit constantly; moment by moment.*

As we were going home, my husband asked what had happened to me. I explained that I had been called to preach God's glorious gospel, a gospel that will set men free from sin and give them a new life in the Father. It is a privilege to be part of the arms extended from the Church.

The only question my husband asked me was, "are you sure?" From that time forward he has supported and helped me in carrying the gospel forth.

What a role for the man to play after being a professional meat cutter who had his own identity, friends and his work that he loved dearly. Many men will never be able to understand this, but if he had not obeyed the Lord and stepped up to walk along side of the calling, I wonder where the ministry would be today?

During this time I shared the calling with my pastor. Many times I can recall the overwhelming feeling to preach His gospel, but not many doors for women were being opened.

If God calls, He will open the doors. He has reminded me of times since then that the doors seem to be closed by men, but He has always opened those I needed to go through.

My pastor allowed me to preach on a Wednesday night, and my first message was "The True Vine." I remember the hunger and anticipation I had to obey the calling on my life. From there, God opened a door for my first revival.

My brother Glenn, which God had delivered from prison, had been called to preach. God later gave him his first church to pastor, the Saint George Church of God. I went there for my first revival on August 11-18, 1989.

I will ever be grateful for my brother and for him seeing something in me God could use and be able to help bring revival to that Church. I have gone back many times even after my brother left to pastor other churches.

Saint George Church of God is a special place where God did many great things. I started that Sunday morning; my husband was still working at that time. He had to leave me that afternoon and go back home.

That was really the first time we had been separated from each other, (except for giving birth to the babies). There was such loneliness that overshadowed me as I tried to get through the revival.

By Monday night I could hardly bare the separation. I had been at the altars that day seeking His face for the service, crying and telling God how much I missed my husband and children. God spoke to me and said if I would obey Him, He would be anything I needed Him to be. I began to cry so hard and said to Him, "I need you to be my husband and children." God came down and touched me in such a wonderful way. I was tried in the fires that day, but God gave victory. I also learned that *"God is more than enough.* To confirm the power of God's Word throughout that revival, listen to how God spoke through one of His godly saints.

My brother had asked one of the saints of God to testify just before I preached. Sister Irene began to cry and say, "God is so very faithful. The enemy has tried to work on me today. I have been tried in the fires but I came out victorious". Needless to say, she preached my message before I did.

I preached concerning gold and how it must go through the fires to be melted, hammered out and shaped. It then becomes a thing of beauty.

May I say to you that when we are hammered away by the enemy on every side, and put in the furnace of fires, we can still come out glowing, (because He has counted us worthy)?

I must share with you that the precious saint of God, Reverend J. D. Shedd, asked me to come to his Church, the Kingsland Church of God. That was my second revival and some doors were slow to open, but God began to work and people started getting saved, healed and delivered. (Then more doors opened).

There have been times when the enemy has pressed so hard and tried to lie to me, but I have kept pressing on. I have never doubted my calling deep in my heart, but there have been a few times when I wondered how I could go on. Men may have doubt about the call of women, but His Word declares in Joel 2:28, *"And it shall come to pass afterward, that I will pour out My Spirit upon all flesh; and your sons and daughters shall prophesy, your old men shall dream dreams, your young men shall see visions."*

To women who have been called, step up and out to fulfill your destiny in God while He is pouring His oil and wine on your heads. Men may doubt, but no one can deny the anointing that breaks the yoke in people's lives.

I have been honored to preach this life changing, God breathed, anointed Gospel for almost nineteen years. I began to get booked in revivals, and God blessed me so much I was booked up two years in advance. I was also honored to be chosen as a lady Evangelist to serve on the State Team in South Georgia, with five men at that time. I am back on the State Team in South Georgia moving into my fourth year again.

God has richly blessed the ministry He has placed in me. I understand that it is not mine, but His. I just get direction from the Captain of the Host and He goes before us and brings total success in every revival.

I have seen the power of the Gospel in revivals as it went to the hearts of the people and convicted, brought salvation, healing and deliverance. We have seen miracles of cancer being healed, deaf ears opened, homes restored and deliverance from alcohol, drugs and homosexuality.

People come into the services with so many problems and, literally, you will see God change their very surroundings right in the midst of His Church.

Once again, His Word declares in Luke 5:31, *"And Jesus answering said unto them, They who are whole need not a physician; but they who are sick."*

Those who are sick seek for an answer and find it when they enter into a fire bought Holy Ghost revival.

I went up to Illinois and ran a revival. The pastor's wife and family were so very special. This man of God, who had labored and prayed for God to do a new thing in His church, saw Him as He came into His Church. God spoke to me in Nashville, Tennessee, where we were spending the night.

He said "there will be miracles in this revival and it will begin with your husband." My husband had a motorcycle accident and had fallen back off it and hit his head. He had burning at the back of his head and there was always a reminder it was there. That Sunday morning God came down into the services, and my husband was the first one to receive his miracle.

One miracle after another began to happen:

Lady healed of Cancer: She had been fighting for her life. God put His hands on her and she receive total healing. About a year later she called just to let me know that God continues to keep her cancer free.

Miracle of a marriage: God instructed me to call a man out in the service, and told him his marriage would be healed. The Spirit directed me to call a woman out on the other side of the church. The Church began to cry and God spoke to her and said, "I will heal your marriage and put it back together." I did not know the man and woman were husband and wife. God did bring a healing in their marriage; several years later I received a letter saying that "God is still faithful to us. Our marriage is better than ever."

Woman That Could Not Have a Child: The doctors had done all they could do for her, and gave the report that she would not be able to have a child. God told her He had heard her prayers and that He would do for her what He did for Hannah. Almost a year later I received a phone call from the couple letting me know that their miracle had just come, a little baby girl. Matthew 19:26, *"With men this is impossible; but with God all things are possible."*

Souls were saved and many more things we will not know until we see Him and then all things will be revealed.

Fires of great deliverance have come into revival and into lives. I was in a church beginning revival at Perry, Georgia. A young man came into the service drunk, had been on drugs and had tried everything, but had not found peace until he encountered Jesus.

At the altar he looked up at me and said, "I heard that there was a "big chick" over here that could get the job done." My mind immediately started thinking, "big chick". Well, he is talking about me! It is quite comical, but as I looked into his eyes I said, "you are right. I am big, and I can't help you but HE CAN" …… I began to pray with him, and he started crying and repenting before the face of God. He received a transformation in his life. He was so drunk in the Spirit, he could not stand up, but left there sober, smiling and understanding that God had worked a miracle in his life.

He looked at the Church and said, "I have tried everything that this world had to offer. I have had no peace, no hope but I have been saved and healed tonight." Praise God, He Still Does……..

I could be here still writing because of the great things He has done time again and again. I never get weary of hearing about what He alone can do…….

What do you do need from Him? Jeremiah 32:27 declares, *"Behold, I am the LORD, the God of all flesh: is there any thing too hard for Me?"*

At this point in my life I was going full time. I was 40 years old when the Lord called me to preach this wonderful Gospel message. It is very exciting, and wonderful to see God as He comes into every service to feed, heal and give the Church true revival.

Let no one tell you it is a life of glamor, fun and excitement to be an Evangelist. I have even heard well-meaning pastors say, "evangelists have it made." They can just go to a Church and stir them up and leave all the mess to me to straighten out. Others remark, "why can't they live by faith? We do."

No one lives more on faith than Evangelists. He or she that is called of God leaves behind family, friends, homes, steady jobs and security. Also very much fatigue comes to the body as you cross the states week end and week out. You never know where you will be sleeping, what situation you may encounter, and you don't know what you will receive in offerings.

In a day where the Church is growing cold and programs have replaced old fashioned Holy Ghost revivals, the gift of the Evangelist is being ignored.

The Bible states very clearly to us in Ephesians 4:11-12, *"And He gave (our Lord does the calling) some, apostles, and some, prophets, and some, evangelists and some, pastors and teachers."*

I have no complaints, because God has been faithful to me. I have not tried to push doors open that God did not want me to go through.

I prayed and sought Him for every service, every message and let Him do the anointing and I followed His leadership and He gave the revival the Church needed.

To be an Evangelist is an honor and calling from God. So to all Evangelists, hold up your head, preach with the anointing and do not let the devil keep you from sharing your gift with the body of Christ. If we are faithful to Him, we will hear Him say one day, "Well done, thou good and faithful servant." No greater words will be heard than these when we stand before Him on that day.

I have served nine and half years in the service of the Lord as an Evangelist. In the middle of 1997, God began to deal with me. He said to my spirit He was going to change my ministry. Where I would go He would already be there.

When I began this book, little did I know what God had planned. The same is true in my life, little did I know that God was preparing me in my mother's womb for great destiny.

CHAPTER 6:

NEW FIELD OF MINISTRY – PASTOR

My younger brother, which had been so instrumental in my life concerning my first revival at
the Church where he was Pastor, and his encouragement,
gave me the strength to go on in spite of things I would
encounter - he had been there.

It was in June of 1997 that he called me and told me
he did not fully understand, but that the Lord said He
was about to change my ministry. The Lord had already
spoken that very word to me. I did not understand at the
time, but at the beginning of 1998, I would become the
pastor of what was at the time Townsend Church of God,
later becoming New Living Water.

In December, the week before Christmas, I was in
revival, and the Holy Ghost spoke to me through tongues
and interpretations. The Spirit said to me, *"I am about to
change the direction of your ministry. I am with you now,
but I will be with you where you are going and I will answer
every question that you have."*

The second message was, *"that men had tried to hinder
your ministry, and even now are trying to, but I will stop*

them. My anointing is upon thee, and I will anoint thee even greater."

I did not know what all God was doing then or has done, but when He sent me to pastor the Church, He gave me a vision for the people and that I was to build a Church; when it was finished there would be an explosion of the harvest fields.

How many of you reading this book knows when God has destiny in your life and you begin to go forth to birth that spiritual baby in the womb, the enemy will come and try to cause abortion to happen?

I became the pastor on January 1, 1998. I was greeted by people I believe had a new determination to help see the plan of God carried out. The man of God, Reverend Robert Edenfield, had been faithful as a servant of the Church for 16 ½ years. He had watched little children who were born during his pastorate become teenagers, and then stepping into adulthood with families of their own. He tended to his flock, and through love and care with tender hands was able to take them to a new dimension in God.

When I walked into the Church, God brought His word forth in my life. We began to see an explosion immediately in numbers and, more importantly, the Spirit.

The enemy started trying to devour the people as a wolf would. I had not even been there three weeks when one of the families in the Church had their house burned down with everything in it.

They were faced with trials in their life, but they were faithful to God, to His house and to his servant and they overcome every battle the enemy brought up against them. The Devil saw that he could not divide us, so he began to try discouragement through the death of several members of the Church.

God sent me there with destiny on my life to help further what the man of God had done under his ministry. God helped me to take the Church to new levels:

1. *NEW GROWTH, NEW BUILDING:*

As a woman I immediately encountered things that a man would not have.

A. I had no understanding on how to build anything. (Not even a shoe box)
B. How does God want His House built on the property?
C. How should I begin? Where would I need to go and who would I need to talk with about finances, building contractor, and all the other things that are to be confronted when building?

Sixteen and a half acres of land was there, it had been paid for and the Church had a CD with $50,000.00 already waiting.

What do I do? God had already given the answer in the revival in December. *'GOD IS ALREADY THERE IN MY DESTINY WAITING ON ME TO TAKE MY POSITION..........'*

For anyone who is in ministry reading this book and God has spoken to you about going forth and you don't understand what, how, and why, HE DOES............

As I began to pray and seek Him, He started revealing His plan for us. Many people may think God does not work in the way I am about to describe, but He does... the rest is history.

I said to the Father, "I don't even know how to begin. Father, you showed the men of old how to build and you

75

will tell me how big it needs to be. Which way do you want the Church to sit on the property?"

While being caught up in the Spirit for almost three hours, God spoke to me. The size will be 72 x 72 in the sanctuary and the Church will sit facing North.

If you and I understand our limitations and what we can and cannot do, we would be further down the road of destiny with God. But, pride seemingly gets in our way. We want men to think that we are the ones that accomplished all of it, but no, it was God all the way.

2. *NEW LEVELS IN THE SPIRIT*:

Praise God, He had helped us accomplish His plan in the building. We had a march from the old Church to the new. It was a journey that would take us into new levels of the Spirit with Him.

God spoke in Joshua 1 that He would go before them and they were to possess what was ahead for them. He would give them courage and strength; He was their God.

I love this. Verse 3 says, *"Every place that the sole of your foot shall tread upon, that have I given unto you, as I said unto Moses."* His promise is still for us. [*It was not God's will that one foot was to rest in the hands of its former owners; likewise, the Holy Ghost intends for everything in our lives to be removed which hinders our progress with the Lord; it is God's will that we possess the entirety of the Promise, which pertains to total victory.*]

God will not force anyone to go in, it is your choice. Your decision does not make the promise any less true. For those who want to experience Him, *YOU CAN*. Waves of His glory were in the house, people were receiving God and coming out of darkness into the light of the Father.

Some people never understand that it is not God's will for them to stay where they started out, whether it has been fifty years ago, or five days. Move into your destiny, and watch the hand of God as He arises to your aid. I am a firm believer that if God calls you to a place, then He will do His part, if we will do ours.

Before we ever placed the building on the property, the Lord dealt with me about anointing the land, all 16 ½, acres and pray over it. I claimed every foot of it for God, to be used for His glory. Little did I know the land was a place where demonic spirits had taken up an abode.

We took the authority that Jesus gave us in His name and came up against everyone of them. I prayed that God would place such a hunger in people's hearts that when they passed by or drove onto the property they would feel His presence. We would later hear those very words spoken. "I don't know why I came here, but I felt something when I drove onto the parking lot." God would bring men and women to His Church and place them in strategic places.

In all the battles and warfare that rise against the Church, you must have people who know how to touch God.

We have watched God intervene time and time again in the midst as we prayed, worshiped and honored Him.

I began to keep a journal on my walk with God as a pastor. I want to share a few excerpts with you.

I say again, anytime there is destiny on your life, the enemy will try <u>to distract</u>, <u>divide</u> and <u>capture you very thoughts</u>, and your heart if possible! He will get you to "major on the minor." Do not allow it, because God has a plan and a future for you. I had faced and dealt with a building program for almost a year and a half in the midst of this, going through the Ministerial Internship

Program in our Church to receive my licenses and also, dealing with sickness in my body.

Sept 3, 1999: I have been on a fast for seven days, I had come into a new level with God and His presence. I wanted to see several things happen:

1. To touch the weariness in the people and lift their heads.
2. I had become discontent with my own self.
3. And after reading the book, "The God Chasers" by Tommy Tenney, I realized I had only touched the surface of what He wanted for me and His Church.

Sept 28,1999: Called for a solemn assembly. I called for the leaders to join with me to go on a fast for three days. We began to pray and ask God to help us, forgive and heal the brokenness.

Oct 1st-2nd: I was called to preach a Ladies Retreat. The great and mighty things God accomplished were so glorious to my spirit. I preached on *"A Divine Appointment For Such A Time As This."*

Oct 3rd: Began revival with an Evangelist that came with the mind of God for the hour for the Church; it lasted four weeks. I saw some of the people take their land and possess what had been lost. Such deep moving of the Spirit.

Since the revival, so many weapons from the devil have come, but God has given the victory through it all.

Throughout the remainder of that year we fought and overcame.

Nov 5th: In my prayer time, God spoke to me that He was calling the Church into a deeper consecration, and we must obey. *"To disobey will bring death in the wilderness for our lives."*

<u>*Nov 12th:*</u> We are marching forward in spite of the enemy.

<u>*End of Year:*</u> God has sent us new people who have been transformed by the Word of God and are moving into a new year.

<u>*2000*</u>: The New Year always brings new hopes, dreams and vows. We vowed unto God and man that things will change in our lives, but they continue as they are. I believe with all my heart we desire it, but never can crucify the old flesh to fulfill it. Look at the definition of <u>*vow*</u>, *"a pledge to fulfill an agreement, a promise."*

The Word of God says in Ecclesiastes 5:4-5, *"When you vow unto God, defer not to pay it; for He has no pleasure in fools; pay that which you have vowed."* (In no uncertain terms, the Holy Spirit told us to be careful about making a "vow." However, if one is made, we are to keep it.) *"Better is it that you should not vow, than that you should vow and not pay."*

In 2000 we again had more people coming into the house in His Presence. There was a young woman that came into our congregation, and I saw in her such potential. She carried things in her life I had longed to see in others I had poured into. I believe she could never really see herself as anything, but God began to work on her and carried her into places in the Spirit and into the heart of the Church.

The year 2000 also carried with it a great tragedy. There was a young woman who was graduating from high school whose name was Carrie. She was an angel sent from God to invade our lives; she had such a smile that would light up any room she came through. She loved me as her pastor, and when she would wrap her little arms around you, everything you had dealt with seemed to just go away.

Carrie had prayer for her family to receive Jesus Christ as their Savior. God came into the service on Sunday and spoke to her. He said, "do not worry about your family for I will save them."

With such a beauty of the anointing, she lifted her little deformed arms and began to weep and worship Him for the promise. Little did we know that on Monday we would receive the tragic news she had just been killed only a block from the Church.

Her dreams of graduation, and plans for her life were laying before her - that is what we thought, but God had other plans. She had just left my daughter-in-law's, getting her hair done for her special day. While at the stop sign, she did not see the logging truck coming toward her, and she drove out in front of it, and was hit head on.

My mind went back to the service the day before and what God had promised. When I went to the family, I met a mom and dad who were devastated.

The questions were pouring out of the dad. "Why? Why? What had Carrie ever done to anyone?" Many questions.

This book is about going through the fires... and God gave them strength to go through the unbearable fires of the loss of a daughter. Little did I know God had prepared me for fires that would be similar to their's, and by God's help, I would reach out with love and compassion, understanding that God is the only One that can carry you through this fire.

Not only did God help me touch them, but the Church arose and ministered to them in their time of distress. IS IT NOT THE HOUR THE CHURCH? Be the life support people need in their hour of fires.

Be a source of strength to those who are broken. Do whatever you can to minister to the families. Though Carrie's battles were over, her family came into the

Church and were great blessings to me. Even as I write this book, I am looking at our curio cabinet and in it is a Bible (a little red Bible) that was given to me by the family, that within itself, is a reminder of God's Divine Love for us all.

Many things in the Spirit transpired in the Church. God began to work in greater moves and His glory would fill the house. When He comes into the house, how many of you know you make a choice? You will either come into greater knowledge of Him and a deeper walk, or you will walk away and out of His presence.

God began to bring more mature Christians into the congregation who were ready to go and possess their promised land. Sometimes God will send people to us who have dealt with major problems and addictions, that they might lead others who enter the doors of the Church to be free.

There is not a Church that has not had its problems, but some go through more than others because of the greater anointing which rests in the place. There have been men and women of God who prayed and believed God that His Church can have all He has given into our possession.

In seven years as pastor of the Church, I went through seven major surgeries. The enemy fought to keep the total prophecy of God from coming to pass. He will take whatever your weakness is and manifest it, and try to destroy your mind, body and spirit, but you and I know that the Word of God declares in 1 John 4:4, *"Ye are of God, little children, and have overcome them: because greater is he that is in you, than he that is in the world."*

After coming through the surgeries, my husband had major surgery also. He stayed in the hospital fourteen days. After coming through so many things, this is the time when the enemy will try to take advantage of your tiredness, and make you believe God must have left you somewhere along the way. It is in this time that we lose sight of the goal, our joy level has been demolished and we cannot even minister as God would desire us to.

I share this with you, because it happened to me, and I believe there are pastors who are dealing with this, too. So many things bombard their minds, they try to get the Church into their destiny, but people will not move. You have become overwhelmed with your situation and the enemy wants you to give up, but take courage, HE IS WITH YOU........

In our times of service to others, we are often forgotten by the same congregation we have labored among. Bitterness, anger, hurt and defeat can get into our spirit and make us ineffective in the pulpit.

I remember one of those days when I had been running from one hospital to another, praying for the sick and trying to encourage those who were struggling.

Most everyone seemed to forget that I was dealing with sickness in my own body, traveling everyday to Savannah to be with my husband through his recovery. I had been tested to the point in my life until I felt stretched without limits. I was feeling a spirit of anger and bitterness creeping into my life. As I was riding to Savannah, I was praying and asking God to touch me. I turned on the radio and Chuck Swindoll was teaching from the life of Moses. He began to say, "I do not know who I am talking to, but you must not allow the spirit of anger and bitterness to get into your life. You will become so upset with the people you are trying to lead, that you will miss your promised land." Moses, that great leader, loved the people but their grumbling, complaining spirits had gotten the best of him and he smote the rock instead of speaking to it as God had said.

God did not let him go into the land of promise; he only got to view from a far off. *"The Spirit of God spoke to me and said you can allow the people to keep you from your promise or you can keep your eyes on me and go in."*

What I did right then was to make a decision that I would not allow carnal people to get me distracted from my destiny with God. Make that choice right now, as a leader, that going where God wants is more important than any person.

I prayed myself beyond my discouragement and struggles into the realm of the Spirit, where He touched me with a fresh new desire to continue on.

In the year 2001, another catastrophe hit us in the church. When I got news about a great tragedy, I arrived at the hospital early that morning where I found a family at their wits' end. The news was regarding their two boys who had been in an automobile accident. As we were waiting to hear the report the doctors would bring, I tried to comfort the family.

The doctors came in to the family, and we went into the chapel where we received the terrible news of the loss of the younger son, 15 year old Jesse. The other son was in critical condition.

This family had known this type grief before, having lost two other children. This is when we must fully trust God that He knows best and loves us.

God had begun to warn the people at the beginning of the year through some messages I preached entitled, "The Danger of Playing With Satan.", "The Hedge of God" and "The Importance of Obedience."

As God tried to reach out to the people, the enemy pressed even harder. God wanted the people to be aware of the devices of the enemy.

Jan 21: I preached on "Tried and Tested Weapons." From that point, the enemy began to undermine the

Word of God, the Message, and the Messenger. I have such a hatred of the enemy. He is a liar and thief, robbing and tying to unclothe the minds of the people of God.

Jan 24: He started attacking the leaders of music. He wants to stop the songs of deliverance and worship from coming.

Jan 26: We are continually praising, praying and seeking God to hold on while the enemy is still raging. He is mad about the Glory coming in the House..........

Feb 11-14: Had revival with a man of God, Reverend Jerry Holt. He came with such authority and anointing to hear from God for the Church. From the beginning of the revival, the devil started. He was bent and determined to bring down anything and everything that God had, but we prevailed through prayer and with the hand of God.

Feb 25th: God help me, I feel as if I am standing all alone. Persecution from the Devil and some of the people. Waves and waves, knocking, trying to bring me down, but His Word in 2 Corinthians 12:9 declares, *"My grace is sufficient for thee; for my strength is made perfect in weakness."*

Feb 28th: We are like warriors traveling through a long hot desert, weary, worn, and so thirsty to see a reprieve from this long, hot war. When we think there is not another push in us or fight left in us, HE GIVES US SUPERNATURAL SRENGTH, to continue on, until we see the finish line.

Mar 13th: I am determined to see God's Church where He wants it to be, that is why the devil hates us so.

Mar 14th: We have been fasting and praying for revival to come on March 18th. As we obey, the enemy brings all his arsenal, but it cannot compete with our armor God has given to us.

Mar 18th: Revival began with Brother Calvin Anderson. He came with such authority and anointing, lifting the people higher and higher into His presence.

Mar 21st: We have continually moved along with our hearts and minds upon the promises of God. Even though it seems at times that God has forgotten us here, we know that He has not.

Mar 22nd: My soul continues to cry out to God for souls. I am like Rachel in the Word of God when she declared in Genesis 30:1, *"Give me children, or else I die."*

Mar 25th: In my times of praying, God reminds me that the land lays out before us, we do not need to be complacent at the very edge of Canaan.

April: I want to always remain sensitive to God's voice and His will for this Church. (I refuse to become another sad statistic of the devil and his works.) I must pass beyond the situations, the looks, and the grumbling, complaining, and look only unto to God, which is the "author and finisher of my faith."

April 15th: Some days are so lonely as I battle in prayer and study. It seems when one problem is solved another one comes up.

April 20th: This is one of the longest wildernesses I have ever been through. I know that there is an end in sight. Lord, help me and the Church to learn the lessons while we are here.

April 24th: I must be careful that I do not let myself get lax and unconcerned.

April 26th: I am trying to lead them into new depths of God. There are few that do not seem to have a real understanding about what true ministry is all about.

April 27th: I watch some of them forgetting where God brought them from. Quick to judge and place their tongues upon the situation of other people's lives. Forgetting that God has forgiven them.

April 28th: I am aware that much has been done to try and demolish our faith in God, in others, and their Pastor. But God will prevail over all of it, if we will let Him.

May 1st: I continue to ask God to give me guidance for the His Church. How can I help to strengthen them, establish them completely in the faith, and a confidence in God that no matter what comes or goes, HE IS ABLE.

May 3rd: I can imagine a little of the loneliness, and discouragement that Moses felt as he tried to lead the people to the place where God had destiny for them to go. Moses is one of the great men of God in the Bible, and the spirit had spoken to me at different times that Moses' spirit was on me.

May 4th: As I began to think about Moses, we basked in the Mount Sinai experience, but that is only a portion of what Moses' life was all about. God trained him in the wilderness, to lead the people with patience, love and concern about their welfare. I am learning that lesson, and I have such a love for my people that God has given to me.

Even now, as I write, the enemy has been plotting against my children. He has often said he would kill my children and take them down, but I have the covenant of God with me.

The Word of God came through again as I was facing this trial, and God gave a Man of God a word for me. He called and said that Isaiah 59:21, *"As for me, this is my covenant with them, saith the Lord: My spirit that is upon thee, and my words which I have put in thy mouth, shall not depart out of thy mouth, nor out of the mouth of thy seed nor out of the mouth of thy seed's seed, saith the Lord, from henceforth and forever."*

It was a word from God confirming His Word with me. In my darkest hour of trials, God never ceases to bring His comforting word to me. In the midst of all the trials, testing, tears and discouragement I still knew that God had a plan for His Church.

If I had gone by feelings and sight of the enemy and all his devices, I would have left, but everyday God would bring fresh manna.

God would remind me of the vision He gave me for the Church. For seven years I remained with the Church and watched God do what He had said.

Remember: *God will only do whatever we allow Him to do.* There was so much more that He desired for the Church, but, like Israel, He will not force Himself on us.

I have tried to share with you just a few of the things I went through as a Pastor, but God was there. It is hard to forget what God really wanted to do. Who knows where the Church would have been if only. *If only* we would obey, God would.

When I left in January 2005, I went with a hope in my heart that people would obey God to the fullest, and to watch Him do what He said He could do. God spoke to me and said, "You have done all that you can." When I left, a part of my heart was left with my people that God had given to me to help them enter into their Promised Land. I continue on with the journey that God started in my life many years ago, to conquer the enemy and enter into my complete destiny.

CHAPTER 7:

MY GRANDCHILDREN

In the midst of trials, God will bring unto you greater blessings. Even when the enemy tries to destroy, God will raise up a generation to carry on a destiny with Him.

God has blessed me with eight grandchildren; they are jewels in my crown. They shine with such potential in their own lives.

May I share with you that the enemy would love to destroy your seed, but he cannot. For out of trouble and sorrow comes fruit.

Remember Leah? She was barren and her sister laughed at her because she bore no children for Jacob. But the Word of God declares again in Genesis 29:31-35, *"And when the LORD saw that Leah was hated, he opened her womb: but Rachel was barren. And Leah conceived, and bare a son, and she called his name Reuben: for she said, Surely the LORD hath looked upon my affliction; now therefore my husband will love me. And she conceived again, and bare a son; and said, Because the LORD hath heard that I was hated, he hath therefore given me this son also: and she called his name Simeon. And she conceived again, and bare a son; and said, Now this time will my husband be joined unto me, because I have born him three sons: therefore was his name called Levi. And she conceived again, and bare a son: and she said, Now will I praise the LORD: therefore she called his name Judah, and left bearing."* When her seed came forth, it produced great things from the womb: *Reuben*, "a son." *Simeon*, "hearing." *Levi* "joined." *Judah*, "praise."

Even when the enemy has tried to destroy what God is producing in your womb, it will bring forth great fruit. The enemy has tried to bring down my children and destroy their lives, but out of my sorrow and pains, God has given me much fruit.

Since the conception of the babies in the womb, I began to pray over them and proclaim greatness in their lives.

Our first is a granddaughter born on February 10th, 1995; her name is Lauren. Her name means, "honor, crowned with laurels, with marks of distinction." She is celebrating her thirteenth birthday, a teenager. I called her my sunshine from the very beginning because when days were overshadowed with pain and darkness, her smile would light up the day. SHE STILL CAN.

Little did I know that God would bless us with seven more sunshines that would light up the night.

Our second is a grandson named Shelby, which is 12, born on August 17, 1995. His very name means, "A Willow, shelter." From the beginning of his birth, I called him my "little gentle giant", not because of his size, but because of his great spirit. His gifts from God are so great; he taught himself to play guitar, can sing and play other musical instruments. Greatness is ahead for him. (Shelby is a reflection of my son when he was that age.)

Our first two grandchildren have such a bonding and love for each other, I believe they will always be closest of friends.

Our third is Corey, who was born on November 11, 1996. Corey's name means, "chosen one." He had such a tough start with sickness, but it has not kept him down. "Chosen one," the very ring of the meaning bring fear to the enemy. I call him, "my little preacher man." He was shy in the beginning, but I see him moving out into new levels.

You see, I have called my grandchildren forth as mighty warriors, preachers, evangelists, pastors' wives, and great lay people to honor their pastors and families.

Our fourth is Chandler, who was born on September 13, 1997. Chandler's name means, "seller." He can sell you on anything because he is very smart. He has blond hair, blue eyes, and when he was born, I put an entry in my journal calling him "the thinker." He is very smart and always has an answer. Who knows what he will begin.

Our fifth and sixth are twins, Sydney and Sophie, born on December 26, 1997. God kept his word with my son when he told him that He would give a double blessing of a very special gift. GOD KEEPS HIS WORD!

Sydney is the more quiet and reserved spirit. Her name means "riverside meadow." She reminds me so much of myself when I was little. I call her, "the quiet one."

Sophie is more outgoing and able to meet people. I call her, "little miss know-it-all." I laugh when I think about the names I gave to them not knowing the meaning of their names. Her name means, "Wisdom and skill." Both have unique personalities and are a joy to watch.

Then our seventh is another little girl named Ashton, who was born on May 7, 1999. She has an independent spirit and thinks she can do it on her own. I call her "my little Gina." She is such a sweet reminder of my own little daughter, Gina. Her name means, "blessed and happy."

Last, but not least, is our eighth, Ethan, born on January 12, 2001. He is called "my little giggles man." When you tickle him under his chin, and he begins to laugh it is the sweetest laugh. He always wants me to shake his head and he giggles, so he can say, "do it again, Nanny." His name means "strength, firmness and long life." As long as he keeps laughing he will have joy to give to everyone he meets.

Eight jewels that are so different in personalities and looks, but pure sunshine that light up the very room. They make you feel so loved, and in their childlike faith, which speaks volumes, let you know you could conquer anything.

We should understand that God did not skimp on any of His blessings, but He has given us the best. That is why I know that my children will arise and be blessed. The devil has plotted, schemed, plundered and robbed ground that did not belong to him through my family, but that ground will be returned to me.

The Word of God says in Hebrews 6:18, *"that by two immutable (unchangeable) things, in which it was impossible for God to lie, we might have a strong consolation, who have fled for refuge to lay hold upon the hope set before us."*

God does not lie to His children, but His promises are *"yea and amen."* I look with anticipation what God is about to do with my family and through them.

God has allowed me the privilege to see in my grandchildren attributes of the Heavenly Father. I am so much aware of the calling upon them.

All of them can sing, Shelby can play the piano, drums, guitar, and while the others are younger, they have been in dramatic plays in the Church. Corey and Ashton are great prayer warriors already in the Spirit, and to watch my prayers being answered is such a wonderful thing to me.

When children have the mind of the Spirit to speak into your life and at the very time when you need strength it is amazing to see the hand of God that you have prayed over them since the time of conception.

I may not live to see them all grown, but I know God is faithful to His promises toward my family, and I can rest with assurance that I have given them my best through prayer and example. God is going to use them all in unique ways to accomplish His plan for His Kingdom. To think that I had a small part in being available to God, I can watch with confidence the God I serve bring much fruit from the wombs of my children.

I am reminded by the Spirit again and again, *"the enemy will be sorry that he ever put his hands on me or my children."* That means all of my seed from generation to generation. Praise the Lord!

CHAPTER 8:

THE BEST TO IS YET TO COME

It has been said that God always leaves the best until last. I do know that Job, God's servant, lost everything he had. It seemed the enemy had won, but God gave the best at the last for Job; twice as much as he did in the beginning.

Job suffered much loss, and one can only imagine the devastation he went through. He said in Job 28:3, *"He setteth an end to darkness, and searcheth out all perfection: the stones of darkness, and the shadow of death."* Job was saying the reason God allows His people to go into darkness and through the fiery trails is because there's treasure in there. God is working to bring out the treasure in us that will last. There are fires deep in the earth that purify and produce precious things in pure form: gold, gems, rubies and diamonds.

You will never find gold nuggets sprinkled around on the ground, that's not where they're produced. They are produced only by the fires and the pressures deep in the earth. When God gets through with us, there will be precious things come forth out of the deep furnace.

The hot fires have caused me to have precious stones produced in me. There are two that I think are worth speaking to you about:

1. *Most Confidence in the God that I serve.* I will never forget the night when at around 3:30 in the morning, a very severe trial came to me. Our middle son was dealing with depression, loneliness and feelings of not being able to be all that God would have him to be, so he tried to drown it all with alcohol. That night, after receiving a phone call from the place where he was, we were instructed to pick him up. I began to weep loudly to God and tell Him I knew I could not handle this anymore, but my Heavenly Father spoke to me and said, *"Cast not away therefore your confidence which hath great recompense of reward."*

I do know if you have had a time in your life when everything seems to be crumbling around you and you did not even understand what was happening, but then God came. I didn't know at the time where the Scripture was, but I got up immediately and begin to search for it and found it in Hebrews 10:35. I wrote at the bottom of my Bible, *"victory was mine from that night forth."*

Did those things begin to turn around immediately? No, but you see I learned to have confidence in God. He is a God who will keep you in the middle of the night. The word confidence means "assurance." There are not many things that you can have assurance in, in a time when all around us things are falling apart, but God can be trusted with all of your heart.

2. *Another stone is that God is fair.* God knows what I need and He has always has my best interest in

His mind.. Even when we struggle with whether He really knows where we are, He is a fair God. What He does is for our benefit that we might see those precious stones buried deep within us that might come forth to touch someone else.

In Psalm 73, David questioned God concerning the wicked and their prosperity. This almost made David stumble spiritually and lose his faith. You and I can get our eyes on people and what seems to be the blessing of the Lord over them instead of us, and cause us to almost lose our faith in God. David said in 73:17, *"Until I went into the sanctuary of God; then understood I their end."* David understood that God is a faithful God and we must leave everything to Him. You and I must learn these valuable lessons, <u>Confidence in God</u> and the <u>Faithfulness of God</u>; we must bring these same stones into the lives of others.

Remember in the Book of *Joshua 4:21-24, "And he spake unto the children of Israel, saying, When Your children shall ask their fathers in time to come, saying, "What mean these Stones?" 22: Then ye shall let your children know, saying, Israel came over this Jordan on dry land. 23: For the LORD your God dried up the waters of Jordan from before you, until ye were passed over, as the LORD your God did to the Red Sea, which he dried up from before us, until we were gone over. 24: That all the People of the earth might know the hand of the LORD, that it is mighty: that ye Might fear the LORD your God forever."*

What is the Scripture stating? Pick up something in your life and carry it with you into the tomorrows and touch someone. Victories, memories of a great battle you won in the strength of God, and give it away to someone. My life should be a light shining in the dark of someone else's life.

Have you been in the darkness? Don't give up now, it may feel darker and more lonely than it has been, but God is working on something. YOUR STORY IS NOT FINISHED YET............ Because You're Best Is Yet To Come!

There is a song *The Inspirations* sing, which is entitled, "The Best Is Yet To Come." When we talk about the best being yet to come, we automatically think about Heaven and all that it has for us. Heaven is a real place that Jesus spoke of in John 14:1-4, *"Let not your heart be troubled: ye believe in God, believe also in me. In my Father's house are many mansions: if it were not so, I would have told you. I go to prepare a place for you; I will come again, and receive you unto myself; that where I am, there ye may be also. And whither I go ye know, and the way ye know."* This is one of those stones that you can depend on. Jesus said it and it will happen, and we know that the best is yet to come.

Look again with me in Revelation 21:3-7 and see why the best is yet to come. *"And I heard a great voice out of heaven saying, Behold, the tabernacle of God is with men, and he will dwell with them, and they shall be his people, and God Himself shall be with them, and he their God."* 4. And God shall wipe away all tears from their eyes; and there shall be no more death; neither sorrow nor crying, Neither shall there be any more pain: for the former things are passed away. 5. And He that sat upon the throne said, Behold, I make all things new, And he said unto Me, Write; for these words are true and faithful."* 6. And he said unto me, It is done. I am Alpha and Omega, the beginning and the end, I will give unto him that is athrist of the fountain of the water of life freely. 7. He that overcometh shall inherit all things; and I will be his God, and he shall be my son."*

And, THE BEST IS YET TO COME: God will be with us, He shall wipe away all my tears, (I have cried until there was seemingly nothing left inside of me) and I can't wipe them away, but He is going to. No more death and sorrow, no crying, no more pain. Praise the Lord. Did you notice verse 5b? *And he said unto me, Write, for these words are true and Faithful.* (Assurance, confidence, and faithfulness.)

AND STILL THE BEST IS TO COME. As my mom was dying, I read to her this chapter concerning the best to come. The glory of God will be there, gates of pearl, streets of gold, no night, no darkness, pure crystal river, fruit trees, but best of all HE WILL BE THERE AND WE WILL BE WITH HIM................... *Verse 3, "And there shall be no more curse, but the throne of God and the Lamb Shall be in it; and his servants shall serve him; 4. "And they shall see his face.* It is what I have been waiting for to see Him and hear Him say, "Well done thy good and faithful servant. Oh, Praise The Lord, the Best Is Yet To Come!!! How glorious this day will be.

A dear young man of God in my congregation named Brother Scott Rozier, penned these words under the inspiration of God; let them speak to your heart as they did mine.

I WILL BE THERE

I wasn't there in Bethlehem,
where in a manger He did sleep
I wasn't there in the temple,
where at twelve He did speak
I wasn't there at the Jordan,
when the Spirit unto Him was sent
I wasn't in the wilderness,
when Satan came to tempt

I wasn't there to witness,
when the multitude was fed
I wasn't at the tomb,
when He raised Lazarus from the dead.
I wasn't in the garden,
where He prayed in agony
I didn't hear Him say,
let this cup pass from me.
I wasn't there on Calvary's hill,
when his precious life He gave
I wasn't there the third day,
when He resurrected from the grave.
But I will be there that morning
eternal bright and fair
When He splits the eastern sky,
and we meet Him in the air.
I will be there to hear Him,
when He says to me "well done"
You have been a faithful servant,
a crown of life you've won.
I will be there with the millions,
as we gather around His throne
To lift up His name with praise
and worship Him in song.
I will be there when the angels
stand back and let us sing
For they can only listen,
because they have not been redeemed.
Yes, I will be there in Heaven,
No pain, no sorrow, no care
Where I'll live and reign forever,
I sure hope to see you there

THE BEST IS YET TO COME RIGHT NOW.

In our churches we will see the greatest move of God we have ever experienced in Revival. The Church will arise with such power and authority that the devil and his Demons' very devices will be turned on him to bring destruction to his kingdom.

Ministers will stand and gain new strength to fight again another day.

Families that have been devastated by the prince of darkness will come together.

Marriages will be restored by the restorer Himself, sons and daughters will be reunited, and we will become the family that God ordained in the beginning in the Book of Genesis.

Those who have had chains wrapped around them from sins of homosexuality, murder, adultery, alcohol, and drugs, will begin walking out of Egypt and come into the fullness of the Father.

People will be in love with Him, with that hot, fervent heat. I believe this is what the people of God can expect. How can we not see it when He is on our side?

My prayer for the reader of this book is that you understand the power of God, and know there nothing He cannot do for you or your family. You need to understand His consistent love for you and me. (You cannot do enough wrong for Him not to love and care about you.) He was there in our past, He is here now in our present, and He will be with us in our future and for eternity. Nothing changes about God, in fact in Hebrews 13:8, "Jesus Christ the same yesterday, and today, and forever."

I pray that as you read, you will be healed from all of your heartaches and pain and take hold of the nail scarred hand of Jesus. I also pray that you will get up and out of the fires that will try and consume you, and, most of all, keep you from the work of God in your life.

I love what A.W. Tozer said in his book, In Pursuit of God. "To the child of God there is no such thing as an accident he travels an appointed way ..... accidents may indeed appear to befall him and misfortune may stalk his way; but these evils will be so in appearance only and will seem evils only because we cannot read the secret script of God's hidden providence."

In other words, everything that happens to us has been orchestrated by the Designer. What a thought, when we are facing the darkest of nights and the fires seem to be heated seven times hotter by the enemy of our souls. The designer has everything under His control working for our best interest. He has a plan and a purpose for our lives and if, He, the Designer of our lives, put us here, He will keep us.

PRAISE THE LORD!!

When I began to write this book, I was in the middle of a fire so hot I thought I would never be able to come up out of it, but here I am expressing to you the greatness of God. Get your eyes on the goal and look up for He is standing with you in and through your fires!!!

HE WILL COMPLETE THE JOURNEY HE HAS STARTED

FINAL PRAYER

Our Heavenly Father, we thank you for allowing your Spirit to give us the inspiration and a heart to understand your will for this book. We pray that every person who reads this will be so touched by your love and strength and will come through their fires. We thank you, Father, that even when the enemy is whispering in our ears, you are not going to make it, we still can rise up and receive victory over the enemy and his cohorts. Thank you, Father, for the peace and healing that you can only send. And thank you, Father, for giving me this book, THROUGH THE FIRES – GOD. I have been renewed in the writing and remembering of the victories you have brought me through. PRAISE IS UNTO YOUR NAME. I know that you are my Heavenly Father, and I have felt your arms around me all my life and am with such anticipation looking to see your face and just love you for eternity ……….. your daughter.

CONCLUSION

I was reminded just recently that you and I are not the first to ever face the fiery hand of the enemy. When we are in the fires we forget that so many others went before to pave the way for us. Read Hebrews 11 and see the fires they went through: put into prisons, unjustly treated, forgotten by men, gave up riches, suffered reproach. They went into literal fires, weakness, torture, mocking, beatings, imprisonment, stoned to death, destitute, afflicted in body and mind and tormented.

When you read about these heroes you think, what did you say about my fires? Thank you: Moses, Abraham, Joseph, and so many others who endured until the end.

And, to my heroes in the faith I would like to say thank you.

Mom, thank you for your true love for your family and all your hard work, and the endless days when no one really knew what you were going through, but you kept moving ever toward Him that is faithful. Rest and enjoy your victory.

My brothers and sister. Thank you for being my family, and even though there have been many times when the fires were so hot and days so long I forgot to tell each one of you just how much you mean to me, I tell you again, I love you…..

To the love of my life, who has been there and seen me in both good times and in my struggles to overcome in the fires. Together we have forged mighty overflowing rivers and fires that seemed to never end. Want the victory be sweet when we are through with this life and we gather over on the other side?

To friends who had their own fires burning but were faithful to Him and to me, John and Amy, Fred and Rhonda, Scott, Billy and Jackie, Mike and Faye, and Mel, "best buddy", friends and ministers too numerous to name but God knows the strength you poured into me. Doug and Alicia, who finished his race not too long ago.

Thank you, Brother Doug for your constant support, fasting, and prayers; they gave renewed strength to keep going on in the fires. Your reward is great, I am sure. How much we miss you!!!!!

The Scripture reminds us in Hebrews 12:1-3, 11: *"Wherefore seeing we also are compassed about with so great a cloud of witnesses, let us lay aside every weight and the sin which doth so easily beset us, and let us run the race with patience the race that is set before us. 2. Looking unto Jesus the author and finisher of our faith; who for the joy that was set before him endured the cross, despising the shame, and is set down at the right hand of the throne of God. 3. For consider him that endured such contradiction of sinners against himself, lest ye be wearied and faint in your minds. 11. Now no chastening for the present seemeth to be joyous, but grievous: nevertheless afterward it yieldeth the peaceable fruit of righteousness unto them which are exercised thereby."*

Several things to take note of here: first, we have so many that endured the fires and gone through them and are cheering us on. Secondly, Jesus is the author and finisher of our faith, who has already endured the fires and shown us the way. Thirdly, this fire will not last always, and will bring such great fruit out of your life so others may see.

Lift up your heads and walk on through the fires for you will not get burned, but will come out shouting the victory.

Most of all I would like to thank you, Father, for giving me the hope to move through these fires and your wonderful arms reaching for me. May all the praise and glory go to you alone.

Printed in the United States
202527BV00002BB/1-183/P